ANTHROPOLOGY AND SOCIOLOGY SERIES
George Eaton Simpson, *Editor*

Man Made Plain

THE POET IN CONTEMPORARY SOCIETY

Was this the poet? It is man.
The poet is but man made plain,
A glass-cased watch, through which you scan
The multitudinous beat-and-pain,
The feverish fine small mechanism,
And hear it ticking while it sings.
Behold, this delicate paroxysm
Obedient to rebellious springs!

—Conrad Aiken, *Ushant*

by

ROBERT N. WILSON

Man Made Plain

THE POET IN CONTEMPORARY SOCIETY

Foreword by Henry A. Murray

HOWARD ALLEN INC., *Publishers*
Cleveland

MAN MADE PLAIN

Copyright © 1958 by Robert N. Wilson

FIRST PRINTING

The Library of Congress catalog entry for this book appears at the end of the text.

Manufactured in the United States of America

To
ARLEENE

INTEREST IN THE SOCIOLOGY OF ART *has developed slowly in the United States, but recent years have seen a considerable increase in the volume of studies and a strong concern about the methodological problems of this field. Robert N. Wilson's study combines sound sociological research techniques with a personal interest in poets and their poetry. His analysis of the role of the poet in American society is exceedingly well-conceived and well-executed, and is invitingly presented. It is a notable contribution to the development of a sociology of art.*

Professor Henry A. Murray's thoughtful Foreword will be stimulating to all who are interested in the relationships among contemporary social scientific research, the criticism of art, and the work of creative artists. Some readers will not agree with all of Professor Murray's commentary on Mr. Wilson's study and on the sociology of art, but all will find it provocative and valuable.

George Eaton Simpson

Oberlin, Ohio
March, 1958

HERE IS A SURPRISE: a talented American sociologist of
the new order who is vocationally concerned with poets
and their ways, and, what's more, who heartfully affirms
that poets have fulfilled, do fulfil, might or should fulfill—I am uncertain which—an important role in contemporary American society.

To be sure, America can take pride in a few sociological schooled minds who have had revealing things
to say about the arts. But these men of the old or of the
old-and-new order are exceptional members of their
chosen discipline as with giant strides it is nowadays
advancing in America. They are exceptional not only in
their genuine enjoyment and understanding of the emotive, mythic language of the arts; but because they write
as social philosophers, historians, or critics, in the grand
humanistic tradition of Europe, viewing, interpreting,
and appraising the objects of their devotion from a
space-surveying and time-surveying cultural height. By
the old dispensation a scholar was free to speak or write
out of the fullness of his life and wisdom, the assumption

being that he had unrecountably experienced on the nerve the best reasons for his judgments.

Today, however, most sociologists of these United States, indifferent to intangibles, have programmatically abjured over-arching apperceptions and evaluations of this sort. Much as the physical and biological scientists, and later the psychologists, sundered their old allegiance with philosophy and planted their faith in emotionless observations and measurements of sense-data, so the sociologists of our time are stressing more and more the need for large-scale researches, for a multiplicity of systematically and impartially recorded facts, and even for miniature experiments, as ground for their theoretical conceptions. Only the elder statesman of sociology are still permitted to indulge in far-ranging utterances without enough evidence to support them, and only out of role are they allowed a few explicit value-judgments, provided these are qualified and cautious.

And so today, when we learn that a young sociologist of the new order has been vocationally concerned with poets and their ways, it can be taken for granted that he has personally interviewed a sufficient sample of this distinguished breed in accord with a prearranged schedule of topics relevant to his aim. This and more is just what Mr. Wilson was the first to do a number of years ago. As free as possible of preconceptions and presumptions, he approached his inviting task in the manner—deferential, tactful, inquiring, and receptive—of one who comes to learn whatever each informant is disposed to tell him.

In this initial, crucial phase of his endeavor, he was remarkably fortunate—in meeting poets of such genius and such willingness—and remarkably successful—in obtaining the facts and the opinions that he sought. The discourses in several instances led to a fructifying friendship and thereby to the possibility of a more intimate inward understanding of the poet's nature. One outcome is the emergence from the womb of sociology of a zealous champion of the poet. In the domain of this emotionally ascetic discipline such zeal is unconventional.

To understand the fervor of his praise—why the author talks as if he felt that literature rather than social science is in need of an eloquent defense—we should keep the fact in mind, with other possibilities to be suggested later, that he is addressing colleagues who have practically excluded art and poetry from their professional thoughts and talk. In view of art's unexampled efficacy down the centuries—the total dependence of Christianity, for example, upon the poets of the Old and the New Testament, as well as upon numberless representors of its sacred myth and sacred figures, in architecture, sculpture, painting, rituals, chants, anthems, hymns, prayers, and poems— and in view of Beauty's high unchallenged place among the values of cultivated persons of the Orient and Occident—in view of so much passionate history and more, the relegation of art to a little disembodied place in today's American science of society is cause for query. Let us see what can be said in a few words.

The over-all objective of sociologists is the construction of a theoretical system in the abstract terms of which one may describe, explain, and predict the course —within a changing environment—of those regulations of those transactions among those specialized activities, which together constitute a society as well as ministering to its members' needs. Sociology as such is not concerned with individuals as such. Particular persons may drop out of a group for one reason or another—resignation, expulsion, illness, death—without impairing to a significant degree its integrity and efficiency, provided they are replaced as usual by almost equally qualified new members. It is largely for this reason that a society is best defined, not as an assemblage of persons, but as a processional system of manifold functional activities, or roles.

Theorists of a young science, such as sociology, cannot deal with everything at once. They must choose a starting place, and the more scientific and feasible place to start is with the study and definition of those specialized endeavors and effects without which no objects of their professional attention—in this case, groups or societies —can endure. In conformity with this judgment, the prevailing disposition in American sociology is to stress the social interactions—in families and in the spheres of economics and of politics, each broadly defined— which are directly or indirectly requisite to the satisfaction of the more urgent somatic, material, affiliative, and power wants of the group's or society's membership. In short, the greater interest is in those material entities and in those instrumental actions and responses which are *extrinsically* most valuable, functional, or practical, in the sense that they most obviously contribute to bodily and social comfort and survival. Most of these activities —which look forward to rewards in the not-too-distant future—are apt to be described as "work," "doing something"—conduct that is obedient to middle-class Protestant morality—, in contrast to activities which are *intrinsically* pleasurable or thrilling—and hence, by this ethic, self-indulgent—, the play of the body, of the senses, of the feelings, of the intellect, of the imagination, of the spirit of faith, comedy, or tragedy.

It happens, to the advantage of social scientists—all of whom, by definition, seek objective uniformities as ground for valid propositions—that most practical endeavors and effects are both overt—and hence most reliably perceived and recorded by trained observers—and relatively uniform, in the sense that they are repeated often with little variation. The probability of this latter desideratum of the scientist is increased by his focusing attention on already established groups during their homeostatic phase of maintenance, when their course is marked by the highest degree of sameness relative to change. More difficult to conceptualize in a legal way are the far less stable phases of formation, growth, and evolution as well as the less stable phases of involution and decay. Furthermore, American sociologists of the new order, disdainful of unfounded speculations, are oriented towards comprehensive, classified collections of data obtained, when possible, at firsthand. By their standards, records from the past are neither sufficiently reliable nor sufficiently complete. Thus the prevalent trend is towards non-historical formulations of existing systems.

Finally, let us note that in their desire to arrive at statements which are most generally valid and applicable, American sociologists have inevitably stressed quantities. Their ideal has been to study the greatest possible number of individuals or of groups and to identify, let us say, the most prevalent beliefs, evaluations, and patterns of behavior. Through the statistical manipulation of numbers obtained from massive investigations of this nature, social scientists are able to arrive at confirmable formulations of dominant (majority) values, aims, and modes of action, as well as of some of their more obvious relationships.

Since the scientist's creed forbids explicit value-judgments, he is not inclined by training and, indeed, not often tempted to affirm—unless it be a question respecting some historical or scientific fact—that in his opinion the majority of his fellow citizens are wrong, or bad, and that a minority are right, or good. For him the more chronic temptation is the opposite of this: initially, by the mere publication of his figures, to nourish the idea in others that what the majority do and say is right, and eventually to lie down with this idea himself and rest with it. The social scientist's susceptibility to this uncon-

scious drag is augmented by the fact that his theories
are statements of probabilities, dependent for their con-
firmation on the predicted behavior of the average or of
the majority of his subjects, and therefore, that the near-
average people who conform to the majority are the ones
who confirm his theories and thus reward his scientific
efforts. In due time, the *confirmists* of scientific laws and
conformists to social customs and opinions become
equated with what is functionally right and proper, with
social adjustment and normality. Anyhow, the inevitable
effect, it seems to me, of the quantitative methods, criteria, and published findings of American sociologists
is to give comfort to the standards of the confident
majority and thus to augment, if anything, the tyranny
of mediocrity, especially by flattering as they do the
already grossly hypertrophied disposition to take some
quantity—such as size, speed, cost, wealth, salary, productivity—as the measure of an entity's or of a person's
worth. "How with this rage shall beauty hold a plea,
Whose action is no stronger than a flower?"

There are, of course, numerous individual exceptions
to this necessarily brief, over-simplified and over-gener-
alized account of the outstanding orientations of American sociologists of the new order; but it may, nonetheless,
serve as a preliminary hypothesis to explain in part why
it is that artists in general and poets in particular are
accorded so little place under the sun of social science.

Since poets do not act as a group in the manufacture
of their wares, they constitute no system of cooperations

of the sort that the sociologist is trained to study. The sociologist's professional intelligence is not engaged by solitaries—renegades, castaways, hermits, anchorites, secluded thinkers, dreamers, Ishmaels, communicants with Nature. It is true that some poets do occasionally join an association but it is not to fulfil their calling that they join it and their attendance at meetings is likely to be casual and irresponsible. It is also true, as detailed by Mr. Wilson, that most of them, under existing conditions, have to earn a living outside their art; but this is another matter. When they are making money they are something else—clerks, insurance agents, teachers, librarians, doctors. As poets they do not minister to their countrymen's most urgent wants; they have no stomach for the complexities of economics; only a very few of them, as amateurs, occasionally engage in politics; and they do nothing to promote the dominant myth of social ascension through material success. In other words—to shorten a long story—American poets in our day, as Mark Twain said of the King of England, are not connected with the works. Does their presence or absence make any measurable difference? Who, if they went on strike for a few years, would notice, feel the lack, register a complaint?

And then, of all classes of persons, poets are among the most irregular and unpredictable, and hence the hardest to pin down conceptually. They are lured by novelty and change, by possible wonders and surprises. With enough cash in his pocket, a poet is free to wander, as many have, over the face of the globe. Any place, any time might be the very place or time for vision or for writing. How can a scientist arrange to catch a poet in the act? And if he did, how could he record it? Poetical activity is secret, imperceptible. It is not what is out there, obvious in a common way to all of us, that makes the poet; it is the sharp selections and discriminations of his senses, his intuitions, his private interpretations of what is there, together with his interior sensations, his peculiar feelings and intense emotions, the span of his constantly combining imagination, his amazing inventions, and, first and last, his unique capacity to compress the essence of his experience into animating metrical arrangements of verbal sounds and sights signifying something that involves us. In short, we see the final product, but we cannot see the intermittent covert processes by which it was produced.

Poets are concerned with intrinsically satisfying forms of emotional experience and the precise qualities of their exciting correlates, and with the musical expression of these careers of feeling, these sentiments, these tastes and/or the pictorial representation of these correlates. They delight themselves in the hope of delighting others, of generating in their readers equivalent emotions and so of sharing and of propagating their experiences, their intuitions, their admirations and aversions. The highest gift of all in poetry, in the telling words of the poet-critic Bridges, is "the power of concentrating all the far-reaching resources of language on one point, so that a single and apparently effortless expression rejoices the aesthetic imagination at the moment when it is most expectant and exacting and at the same time astonishes the intellect with a new aspect of truth."

No doubt a somewhat different emphasis is required to describe the typical experiences, purposes, and accomplishments of the majority of poets in this science-dominated age of impressive technical inventions and coolly calculated tactics. Disillusioned and self-depreciative after its cultural defeat by the deaf and deafening massive forces of this century's mechanized Philistines and with nothing significantly new to say after more than a hundred years of passionate metric utterances, the heart—except in faithful Aiken and a few others—has ceased to be the poet's argument. But, in spite of this and more, it seems to me that one may distinguish the poetic from the scientific enterprise by stating that the poet down the ages has been preoccupied with concrete, emotive presentations of internal, central, subjective, existential, evaluative truth, knowledge of his self and its reactions, knowledge of the *feel* of things, of pain, grief, desperation, joy, love, and ecstasy. In contrast, the social scientist of the new order is preoccupied with abstract (mathematical, if possible), referential presentations of external, peripheral, objective, positivistic, non-evaluative truth, knowledge of the uninvolving *look* of things. It is the difference between *being* in love (and saying it in a sonnet) and witnessing with cool eyes the *doings* of a lover (and reporting them conceptually). Of this nature roughly is the vocational gulf between poet as poet and social scientist as scientist, the bridging of which has become especially difficult of late because of extreme refinements of uncommonplace special symbolisms, by the poets, one the one hand, and by the scientists, on the other.

Since Mr. Wilson devotes several pages to an exposition of these two contrasting languages as initially expounded by Ogden and Richards, Suzanne Langer, and others, I shall leave this affair to him: Here I am merely pointing to the widely reproached, half-purposeful "unintelligibility" of modern poets as one of the many reasons why they have been shunned by sociologists of the new order. Another related reason is the necessary sensitiveness and elusiveness of poets and their not unfounded suspicion and antipathy respecting the social scientist's (especially the psychologist's) lethal jargon, his crass instruments of inquiry—of which Auden warns—, his crude invasions of privacy, and his reducing analyses which supposedly explain away the distinctive worth of poetry as form.

And finally—to end this enumeration of factors which have made the poet an unfeasible object of sociological attention—there are so few poets, poets of the calibre interviewed by Mr. Wilson. In the statistician's columns they add up to so small a figure that, if the great objective is to discover and define the dominant patterns of our culture, what today's poets say and do can be left out. Measured by the preferred instruments of this youth-

ful, physics—emulating science, poets are of no obvious
account. Why should a sociologist attend to them?

Does a non-historical sociologist have to make some
abstract place in which to put the documented fact that
the greater poets through the ages—Homer, Aeschylus,
Sophocles, Virgil, Dante, Shakespeare, Racine, Goethe,
and a host of others—have been venerated as much as,
if not more than, the most eminent of any other calling,
that no immortality is comparable to the perennial magic and enchantment, the imperishable wisdom of the
best poetic prose and verse? Must a really modern sociologist take account of the mutitude of portraits, busts,
and statues of the poets, the boulevards, streets, squares,
buildings that commemorate poetic power? Does a
sociological economist have to count the price of hand-
some editions of the poets, total the thousands of dollars
paid at auctions—even by uncultivated, just-arrived
American tycoons—for a single original manuscript, early
folio, or letter of a poet, the cost of an autograph, of a
lock of hair, of anything, indeed, that one of them used
or owned, or the amount of money that is spent in travel-
ing to a poet's birthplace, home, or grave? Must a sociologist acknowledge the capacity of a few distinguished
poets, even of one world-honored voice, to elevate the
native pride, the self-respect, of an entire nation? Is it
necessary that a student of current language and communication take note of the invention and diffusion of
impressive—tart, pungent, lusty, telling—phrases, of the
multiplicity of clichés that were once novel creations of
a poet, take note of the number of times at a demanding

instant in a document or speech some poet's tongue provides the exactly apt expression? Should a behavorial
scientist's account of his society include the recreations of
its members, their imaginative delights? And if so, is he
either permitted by his creed or fitted by his training to
evaluate the quality of their literature, the standard of
their passions, the level of their tastes, the perfection
of their art of living? Anyhow, is a democratic sociologist,
with proper respect for the majority, the common man,
the masses, well-advised to devote much time and
thought to a little class of esoteric persons, an elite group,
a happy or unhappy few, a small exclusive fraction of
the creative minority of his nation?

Whether or not these questions are answered in the
affirmative, the fact is that Mr. Wilson, a disciplined
sociologist, has had what it takes to overcome the bulk
of the handicaps enumerated in this foreword, to embark
on this preliminary study of a sufficient sample of today's
poets, and to complete it with competence and devotion.

I would regard this book as a good omen. It raises the
possibility that a few of the author's specially gifted and
enlightened colleagues may see fit to follow suit, to un-
dertake further studies, not only of our living poets but
of their living works, and thereby to correct eventually
the present unavoidable lopsidedness of their discipline.
Then, in so far as changes within the province of sociology affect the surrounding atmosphere of values, our
world should be a better place in which to breathe and
hope.

But this volume is more than a good omen, more than

a promise of benefits to come; it is a benefit here and now in giving us a good look at poets of our time through the social scientific lenses of a particular explorer. This look is capable of teaching us something about the poets, a little something about the lenses, something about the explorer, and, finally—by noting differences—, more than a little about ourselves and our own lenses.

Mr. Wilson's focus of concern is the career in role of the poet in contemporary American society. What special dispositions and abilities does he manifest? What uniquely valued aims and hopes sustain him? How does he view himself as craftsman? How does he prepare, make way, for those capricious influxions into consciousness, those illuminations, upon which his whole endeavor hangs? How does he work? It is the poet, the poetic process, then, rather than any finished works of art, which is this volume's theme.

The principal professional lens through which Mr. Wilson views his poets is the concept of role, indispensable to both sociology and psychology. So far as I can see, there is no possible substitute for this concept, but, as conventionally employed, it cannot be readily fitted to the poets of our day. Common usage allows us to define a role by listing the set of functional effects which a person occupying a particular status, or position, *should* achieve (definition 1), or by listing the set of functional effects which a person occupying this position actually *does* achieve (definition 2). When a social system is operating happily and effectively, without serious antagonisms, strains, or frictions, definition 2 corresponds to definition 1. Each member of the group does what he should do, at the proper place and time, in the proper manner, and in relation to the proper person. Sociologists define informal as well as formal roles, but do not include, within the limits of this concept, the privately satisfying and beneficent effects of *doing* on the doer, of sleeping on the sleeper, of eating on the eater, of swimming on the swimmer, of creative writing on the writer. One does not say that a man's role is to survive, to *be,* to enjoy life, to *become,* to ripen, to perfect himself. Thus leisure, the summum bonum, is accorded no official place. Also excluded are the dysfunctional, or hurtful effects of an activity, either on others or on the actor himself. Here, perhaps, is where the greatest difficulty lies, since the status-quo-maintaining-and-defending activities of an inflexible conformist (holding to the literal text of definition 1) may be exceedingly dysfunctional from an evolutionary point of view, whereas the staus-quo-upsetting activities of a nonconforming critic of society, although temporarily hurtful, may prove functional in the long run. This dilemma must certainly be faced in dealing with poets as a class, one of whose functions, in Matthew Arnold's view, is to indict the mechanizing and brutalizing effects of our industrial, materialist society. Is a sociologist in a position to agree that a poet *should* attack his culture (definition 1)? Or has he sufficient scientific data to affirm that the poet's attacks have been, to any appreciable degree, successful (definition 2)?

To discover what set of functions a position-occupant *should* successfully perform, one asks those who are most affected by what he does and/or have some reason to believe that they are justified in stating what he *ought* to do. Thus, by definition 1, a role consists of those actions which are expected or required of a person, say, by most of his superiors, by the majority of his associates or neighbors, or by the general public. Since there is rarely a veritable consensus among role-definers of such different classes, or even among role-definers of a single class, and rarely a consensus in respect to the reasons that they give (custom, law, compact, morality, logic, authority, revelation, etc) to justify their expectations or demands, this definition of a role in actual practice consists of a number of different, partial definitions. But even after amending in this way the meaning of the concept, its utility in the formulation of the poet's office is certainly not obvious.

How can we apply it to a free person, to someone who, in a typical case, is professionally employed by nobody, adequately paid by nobody, beholden to nobody, and, hence, is under no compulsion to satisfy anybody but himself? Who, in this entire nation, has the *right* to say what such an individual must do? And, if nobody has this right, if nobody can require anything at all of him as poet, from whom can a sociologist obtain the information that is necessary to conform with definition 1?

Many people hope that the poet *will,* or even believe
that the poet *should,* do one thing or another for them
—amuse, inspire, or console, or feed their love of nature,
region, country, or religion, or provide a mythology or
faith to live by. But the modern poet, feeling in no way
obligated by such hopes or such demands, makes no
effort to comply with them. If the intuition moves him,
he will tell us in words that cannot easily be dismissed
that all of us are hollow men existing impotently and
ignobly from day to day in a spiritual Sahara. The public have not asked or wanted him to raise the level of
disgust or of despair by giving utterance to insights and
prophecies of this temper, and so, according to the majority definition of his role, the poet is neither fulfilling
it nor anxious to fulfill it. Indeed he is doing the exact
opposite. But actually, since the public are not led by
education or by experience to anticipate any gratifying
throbs from the best poets, the sociologist can find no
ground for a popular definition of their function. In
brief, the most that one can do with definition 1 is to
limit it to the *hopes,* the multifarious hopes, of the readers and would-be readers of modern poetry, the only
people who need and hunger for emotional transactions
with the poets through their verses. Of those hopes we
have but little exact knowledge since no one, venturing
to explore the minds of the poet's small and select audience, has revealed to us their character and tenor. One
would surmise that the people who are most dependent
upon poetry are those who make space for Aristotle's

highest form of happiness, the contemplative life, defined for later generations by Oscar Wilde as "the life that has for its aim not *doing* but *being,* and not *being* merely, but *becoming."*

According to definition 2, a poet's role consists of the functional (pleasurable, or pleasurable and beneficent) effects which his poetry actually achieves. These effects are in the nature of transient evocations or recurrent raptures of the aesthetic imagination, emotional arousal and catharsis, and possibly—in countless but now often disparaged or disregarded instances—revelation, enlightenment, affectional extension, exaltation. This corresponds to one of the four age-old classes of conceptions of poetry, the class dating from antiquity (e.g. Horace's *delectare, movere, prodesse)* which stresses, besides pleasure, the sensitizing, refining, integrating, educating, ennobling, or civilizing aspect of poetic works. Although no broad detailed study has yet been made of such diverse possible effects of poetry upon different types of readers, casual and devout, there nevertheless is a vast critical literature on the subject to which important additions have been made in recent years. It is partly from this source and partly from his own responses that Mr. Wilson has derived his knowledge of how some people have been excited, moved, and changed by some poets (close to definition 2). With this he has combined all that the poets told him about their own conceptions of their role (definition 3).

In discussing the traditional powers and effects of the

genus poet, Mr. Wilson gives us the impression—flattering to his recent informants—that these functions are actually achieved by the poets of our age (not merely expected of them or intended by them), although he knows as well as anyone that there is no confirming or disconfirming scientific data on this point. Moreover he is certainly no stranger to the fact that the bulk of modern verse is addressed to, or, if not this, is only fully understood and relished by an uncommonly small number, a fastidious clique of specialists. Today's poetry is not for the enthrallment and fruition of the artistic temperament in whomsoever it may dwell.

It is no news that the majority of our most respected poets have been engaged in carrying forward a necessary, though disquieting revolution of speech, style, and feeling. They have done this through a procession of bold syntactic experiments, of radically new conjunctions of words and images, of strange symphonic innovations, and of startling assimilations of material previously excluded as "unpoetical." In interdependence with these endeavors, some of our more eminent critics and poet-critics have been performing sharp, minute dissections of poetical productions, as well as speculating, debating, legislating about the nature of poetry and revising the old rules relative to the absolute necessary properties of a good poem. The unhappy, but no doubt inevitable concomitant of this rapid, largely technical and intellectual development has been a marked shrinkage of the poet's potential audience, potential influence, and hence contemporary function. This state of affairs—so deplorable to those who care for excellence—raises a hornet's nest of questions. How did it come about? Are the poets at fault? Is Western civilization to blame? Is the trend likely to continue? Can anything be done to check or to reverse it?

One would hardly expect questions of this character to be posed by Mr. Wilson, sociologist of the new order. Not only would their serious consideration require judgments, however tentative, on matters that belong outside his professional domain, but not all of these judgments could be wholly complimentary both to his culture and to his poets. Anyhow, like a good scientist, the author has restricted himself to a sympathetic report and formulation of what he learnt from the literature and from the poets individually. One would guess that he is on excellent terms with his society; that his own private experiences with poetry have been gratifying; that he is wise enough to know that a relatively short sojourn in a foreign country does not provide sufficient basis for consistently valid estimates; that on this particular visit he was so hospitably entertained and generously informed by the aristocrats of the country that after his return, gratitude and courtesy moved him to the composition of a book that has the savor of an appreciative bread-and-butter letter; and, finally, that he is eager to incite affection and respect for modern poets among his scientific colleagues. If this last guess be approximately true, it might serve to explain his having drawn the poet's personality, his characteristic traits, as near to the social scientist's personality as the facts allow. In any event, Mr. Wilson has contributed new knowledge to his discipline in this well-written book. It is a firmer, less pretentious, and hence better book, I think, than you would find before you now if some reckless curiosity had goaded him to ask and then to cope with such questions as the following:

Does the sorrowfully narrow influence of modern poets indicate a temporary or even a more permanent retraction, a drying of the springs of hope, passion, and fecundity? Will the poetic part of man, as time goes on gradually turn pale, wither, and close up from lack of feed-back, hanging on thereafter as an atavistic vermiform appendix in the body politic? Was Shelley right, a century and a half ago, in his "Defence of Poetry," when he claimed that: "The cultivation of these sciences which have enlarged the limits of the empire of man over the external world, has, for want of the poetical faculty, proportionally circumscribed those of the internal world." With the best poets in virtual retirement, encysted and estranged, are not many of us Americans suffering from a deficiency disease, a kind of spiritual scurvy, without knowing the precise nature of our malady or how the poetical imagination in verse or prose could contribute to its cure? Is it true that the artistic fibre, the love of beauty is, at best, but meanly nourished and, at worst, desiccated, fractured, and annulled by the ethos of our society? Are not possible young readers more likely to be cultivated to the shoddy artifices of advertising, to the cynically contrived language of the mythology of big industry and commerce? Or, are we perhaps mistaken about the poet's loss of verve, his withdrawal, his retreat, his indifference to us all? In truth, is he not religiously fulfilling his appointed task, that of picturing the average human situation, the present estate of man? Has he not portrayed, over and over again the emptiness, the aridity, the de-humanization, the corruption, the hypocrisy, the deterioration, the schizophrenia, the hopelessness of modern man? Have we stopped reading him because we have no appetite for this verdict, true as it may be? And then, since the advertisers and the sentimentalists, intent on mass seductions, have spoiled so many of our once cherished words, should not responsible writers be obscure until they have made a language one can use without spiritual embarrassment? And is it not probable that the evolutionary role of modern poetry will be fully acknowledged by posterity when its wonders are experienced on the pulses of our better prepared descendants? In any event, are not the experimentalists of today fashioning more exact and honest, tougher yet more supple, less vague, less prettily artificial modes of germinal expression? Are they not inventing a greater range of forms and symbols for the use of creative spirits in the future, who, reared in an atmosphere of debased speech, might be tongueless in their absence? Is there any possibility that some of the poets of our age are, by different paths, converging towards a cyclic myth of being and becoming which will supplant the deceased myths of Christianity and make life meaningful once more? Or, is a mythology something which no poet can generate out of his own heart's brew, though only he is capable of powerfully celebrating its emergence and of drawing all things to it by his magic?

Henry A. Murray

Cambridge, Massachusetts
February, 1958

ACKNOWLEDGMENTS

This book is largely the result of the guidance and inspiration of Henry A. Murray, who first encouraged me to tackle the problem and then supported me faithfully throughout my work. Humanist, psychologist, himself a gifted critic of Melville, he took pains to show me, as he has shown so many other students, that art and imagination are intrinsic to the sciences of human behavior.

Talcott Parsons was influential in developing my ideas about the artist's social role, and has been a kind and perceptive critic. I owe the impetus for Chapter II, on poetic language, to Charles Morris. My general interest in the sociology and psychology of literature was first stimulated by Harrison C. Coffin's lectures on comparative literature at Union College.

My colleagues at the Harvard Psychological Clinic were a source of comfort and wisdom during the early days of research, as have been my associates in various activities during the past several years. To mention but a few of the many friends who have been willing to discuss the poet, and from whom I have learned a great deal: Josephine Murray, Gardner Lindzey, the late Mortimer Slaiman, Robert Harlow, Ralph Patrick, Arthur and Virignia Vidich, Alan Gowman, Joseph Casagrande, Joseph Kahl, and John Gardner.

To the Center for Advanced Study in the Behavioral Sciences and its Director, Ralph Tyler, I owe the precious gift of time which enabled me to rethink and rewrite the entire manuscript. My co-Fellows at the Center have provoked important second thoughts and afforded a critical sounding-board. Of special value have been the comments and questions of Harold Wilensky, Hans Speier, Sherwood Washburn, John Roberts, Kimball Romney, and H. Stuart Hughes.

Miriam Gallaher has been a most perceptive editorial consultant, carefully and ably criticizing the entire manuscript.

Typing and secretarial assistance have been ably provided by Virginia Cass, Marjorie Ingalls, and Joan Warmbrunn.

The poets themselves were of course the most important source of understanding and the true basis of the study. The names of those who gave so graciously of time and energy are listed below. I should note the special help I have received from Conrad Aiken, Malcolm Cowley, and the late Merrill Moore, who have been both luminous in criticism and staunch in practical support, especially in introducing me to their fellow writers. Several literary men, not primarily poets, have been extremely helpful in conversation about the problems of this book. I think particularly of Van Wyck Brooks, the late Bernard de Voto, Konrad Heiden, Lewis Mumford, Gerald Noxon, and Thornton Wilder.

My deepest gratitude goes to the following poets, whose tolerance and enthusiasm were crucial:

Leonie Adams
Conrad Aiken
John Ciardi
Malcolm Cowley
Gene Derwood
Richard Eberhart
Dudley Fitts
John Hay
John Holmes
Randall Jarrell
Weldon Kees
James Laughlin

Robert Lowell
David McCord
Marianne Moore
Merrill Moore
Charles Olson
May Sarton
Winfield Townley Scott
Karl Shapiro
Louis Untermeyer
Richard Wilbur
Oscar Williams
William Carlos Williams

For permission to quote various passages and to use selected lines from the following sources, the author gratefully acknowledges the kindness and courtesy of:

Conrad Aiken and his publisher, Duell, Sloan & Pearce, Inc., for one of the poet's early fragments and also its partial use as the title of this book. The fragment is reproduced on the page preceding the title page of this volume and has previously appeared only in *Ushant*, copyright 1952 by Conrad Aiken, by permission of the author and Duell, Sloan & Pearce, Inc.

Gordon W. Allport: "Personality: A Problem for Science or A Problem for Art?" from *Revista de Psihologie*, 1938, 1-15.

ACKNOWLEDGMENTS

Matthew Josephson for his *Portrait of the Artist as American,* copyright 1930 by Harcourt, Brace and Company, Inc.

Journal of Aesthetics and Art Criticism: "Literature, Society, and Personality," by Robert N. Wilson, Vol. 10, No. 4, June, 1952.

Alfred A. Knopf, Inc.: *Art and Artist* by Otto Rank, copyright 1932; *The Captive Mind,* by Czeslaw Milosz, copyright 1953. Both copyrights by Alfred A. Knopf, Inc.

The Macmillan Company: "Poetry" from *Collected Poems* by Marianne Moore, copyright 1951; *The Poet as Citizen,* by Sir Arthur Quiller-Couch, copyright 1935; "Adam's Curse" from *The Collected Poems of W. B. Yeats,* copyright 1951. All copyrights by The Macmillan Company.

New Directions: "A Pact," "The Rest," and "Salvationists," from *Personae, The Collected Poems of Ezra Pound,* copyright 1926 by Ezra Pound; *The Pisan Cantos* by Ezra Pound, copyright 1948 by Ezra Pound; and "A Reason for Writing" from *The Paradox in the Circle* by Theodore Spencer, copyright 1941 by New Directions. All reprinted by permission of New Directions.

Hermitage Press: "The Nature of Insight" and "The Period of Frustration in Creative Endeavor," by E. D. Hutchinson from *A Study of Interpersonal Relations,* ed. Patrick Mullahy, copyright 1949 by Hermitage Press.

The New York Times Book Review and Donald Barr for the latter's review of *The Horse's Mouth* by Joyce Cary, in the issue of January 29, 1950.

Partisan Review: "A Prize for Ezra Pound" by William Barrett in the issue for April, 1949 and "The Question of the Pound Award" in the issue for May, 1949.

Prentice-Hall, Inc.: *Signs, Language and Behavior,* by Charles Morris, copyright 1946 by Prentice-Hall, Inc. "The New Criticism and the Southern Critics," *A Southern Vanguard,* copyright 1947 by Prentice-Hall, Inc.

Psychiatry: "Poetic Creativity" by Robert N. Wilson, Vol. 17, No. 2, May, 1954, pp. 163-176.

Random House, Inc.: "Under Which Lyre" from *Nones* by W. H.

xxxix

R. N. W.

Cambridge, Massachusetts
November, 1957

xl

Table of Contents

Introduction

SEVERAL YEARS AGO I set out on a rather audacious program of research which involved subjecting a number of poets and other writers to a psychological test. The purpose of the test was to find out as much as possible about the way the creative imagination works. I learned very little in this enterprise that could be construed as reliable psychological knowledge, if by knowledge one means certain uniform characteristics of the poet's personality or his pattern of growth. Nevertheless this effort did yield interesting insights into artistic behavior, and, more important for me, set me off on the quest for a deeper understanding of the process by which a poem is made and of the kind of life poets live in contemporary America.

I then interviewed as many poets as I could, asking them how they wrote their poems and how they viewed the poet's task. Fortunately, most of the writers I approached refused to heed Auden's wry dictum:

Thou shalt not answer questionnaires
Or quizzes upon World-Affairs,

> Nor with compliance
> Take any test. Thou shalt not sit
> With statisticians nor commit
> A social science.

On the contrary, I enjoyed fine cooperation in my search for understanding why and how the poet does as he does. More, I experienced a spiritual generosity and hospitable disposition that not only helped me comprehend the poet but enriched my own life. This, then, is really the book of the contemporary poets who were willing to talk long and entertainingly about their work and their place in our society. While I have drawn on whatever wisdom was available in these matters, my account is mainly built on the poets' own statements.

I would obviously not have dared write about people whose craft is already so well-known to literary critics, editors, and very many literate readers unless I had felt two things: that the detached outsider trained in the study of human behavior might contribute some little perspective to the venerable problems of the artist and his society; and that the poet's voice is an important one, too much neglected by the professional student of behavior and by modern society as a whole. My aim is to demonstrate that the poet is not an exotic creature who properly speaks only to other poets and omniscient critics, but a human and humane artisan, of one spirit with ourselves, who lives vigorously in the real world and writes to all of us about his experiences with the bloody angles and beautiful symmetries of life.

The artist is, to be sure, an exceptional individual; the generality of men have neither the talent nor the determination to follow what is perhaps the most demanding vocation any human being can pursue. But poets are not, as they are so often pictured, an arcane breed whose concerns are remote from the familiar thoughts and feelings we all know. The poet is everyman heightened and refined by a deep longing, a longing to achieve an exact knowledge of self and environment and to express that knowledge in precise language. He magnifies the characteristically human desire to make fundamental sense out of the stuff of experience. In his persistent, almost savage exploration of the self and its relationship to the universe—a universe ranging from Marianne Moore's garden toad to the cosmic reaches of religion and mortality—the poet responds to the civilizing imperative to increase one's awareness. This imperative to expand consciousness, to plumb the nuances of existence, applies with equal force to us all insofar as we claim to be truly human. The poet happens to be quite a bit better than most at the common chore.

The poet knows the world in order to feel it intensely. Most men in modern society know the world in order to manipulate it. Our science, our commerce, our popular culture all press toward the instrumental and the extrinsic. In this climate the poetic impulse is seldom acknowledged. The lust after short-run purpose leads us to neglect both the immediate (it is, after all, already here) and the eternal (it is not scheduled in the apparent future), and thus to neglect poet and saint, painter and philosopher, whose correct devotions are to immediacy and eternity. Hans Speier has phrased the situation in unmistakable terms, in words which carry a right overtone of anger:

> Who is the poet? We are hardly prepared to learn or inclined to believe that the poet is the forgotten You and I who know of nature before it is tortured. In the poet we crucify that part of ourselves which reminds us of knowledge we have forfeited, that knowledge of nature which does *not* enable us to change the world around us but to understand it and live in it.

One other pitiable mistake is today usually committed by those who look, but not hard enough or long enough, at the poet. As damaging an error as the notion that the poet is somehow set apart from the concerns of real life is the related fallacy that he plays a fanciful and irresponsible word-game, limited, moreover, to some foreign province of the language. Nothing could be less true of the serious modern poet. He does indeed play a word-game, but it is a game marked by high seriousness and crushing responsibility in which the stakes are the very life and breath of language. The poet is bound to a morality which demands strict honesty in the reporting of experience and iron resolve to write the report in the best—for him the *only*—possible words. As John Ciardi has said in his superb essay, "The Morality of Poetry":

> Without the poets to guard the language it

would fall apart in the mouth, and with it the
very possibility of social communication. When
a language falls apart a nation is finished.

Ciardi emphasizes that the poet must care enough to
use language only in the most alert and exact way, and
that this caring is part of his devotion to the plain hard
work of doing the poet's job well. That job includes
close observation, tortured thought, exquisite feeling,
and a determination of tongue: an attentive life, full of
joy but full of care. In accepting the high challenge imposed by experience, in responding to life in a manner
both orderly and lovely, the poet knows that he takes
on a job of divine difficulty and devilish frustration.
Yeats tells us, and in telling us he exemplifies the artist's
devotion:

I said, "A line will take us hours maybe;
Yet if it does not seem a moment's thought,
Our stitching and unstitching has been naught.

"Better go down upon your marrow-bones
And scrub a kitchen pavement, or break stones
Like an old pauper, in all kinds of weather;
For to articulate sweet sounds together
Is to work harder than all these, and yet
Be thought an idler by the noisy set
Of bankers, schoolmasters, and clergymen
The martyrs call the world."

And thereupon
That beautiful mild woman for whose sake

There's many a one shall find out all heartache
On finding that her voice is sweet and low
Replied, "To be born woman is to know—
Although they do not talk of it at school—
That we must labour to be beautiful."

Literature, Society, and Personality

CHAPTER I

In the order of thought, in art, the glory, the
eternal honor, is that charlatanism shall find no
entrance; herein lies the inviolableness of that
noble portion of man's being."
— St. Beuve

Anna Sergeyevna was silent for a little. "And
so you haven't the least artistic feeling?" she observed, putting her elbow on the table, and by
that very action bringing her face nearer to
Bazarov. "How can you get on without it?"
"Why, what should I need it for, may I ask?"
"Well, at least to enable you to study and
understand men."
— Turgenev, *Fathers and Sons*

THE RELATIONS BETWEEN LITERATURE AND LIFE have long
been a matter of debate among writers, critics, and other
students of society. Extreme positions have ranged from
the view that literature is the highest, most intense expression of human activity, embracing the most important issues, generating and reflecting all that is vital
in the intellectual and moral world, to the contrary

claim that novels and poems are merely entertaining ornaments which have no solid connection with the mundane universe of operating social and economic forces. But these may be readily seen as false alternatives, distracting our attention from the central task of exploring the various relationships which may exist between the arts as characteristically human enterprises and the diverse other facets of behavior. Neither the acts of writing or reading, nor the content of literary works themselves, ever stands in a simple, direct connection with other areas of life. Literature is not a mirror or a psychoanalytic document, or a report on the state of the nation, although it may indeed contain elements of all these and more. A great book, or even a good book, is a vision of the author; yet it is no longer solely his, since the writing and sharing have endowed it with a kind of independence, a content in and of itself.

Avoiding, then, the temptation to reduce literature to some easily–scored instrument in the social concert, it is appropriate to question the interplay among arts, artist, audience, and the general fabric of life. The newer studies of man—the social sciences—have tended to neglect the arts. In part, this neglect is precisely due to the complexity of the interplay, the great difficulty of counting or measuring or validly assessing the role of creative and appreciative activity in the individual personality or the social pattern. Art-blindness has resulted in a foreshortened model of the human being and a grey-toned, pedestrian portrait of society. The desire to

2

simplify and reduce behavior to its minimum terms has led the psychologist and sociologist to attend almost exclusively to activities, like child–rearing or industrial organization, which seem somehow more tangible than the arts. Artistic creativity and aesthetic experience, those uniquely human and distinctively civilized concerns, have been shunted off as trivial and superficial.

The disregard, and even pronounced animus, shown by social scientists toward art is undoubtedly caused in some degree by their need to separate themselves from an "unscientific" humanist tradition. Only recently emancipated from philosophy and theology, and proudly striving for a rational, empirical approach to social events, the student of man feels obliged to disavow the unsystematic perceptions of poet or playwright. Brusque manner and awkward expression are the outward signs of scientific respectability; and the morning coat of the humanities must be renounced for the shirtsleeves of the laboratory physicist. Poetry, drama, the novel, no matter how brilliant their insights, have been judged to present no "true," verifiable statement of the human condition; nor have the making and receiving of artistic creations been credited with forceful implications for men's actions.

One may now hopefully detect certain changes in this attitude. The concern with language as a mold of human experience and a vehicle of social intercourse is leading the student of behavior toward some commerce with poetry and literary criticism. The growing recognition of man as builder and inhabitant of a sophisticated symbolic environment is directing attention once more to the philosopher and artist. As undeniable facts of contemporary life, increased leisure and education are compelling us to look with renewed vigor at creation and recreation as distinctively human forms of serious play.

Literature as a Descriptive Technique and Source of Knowledge

In its broadest sense, literature may be viewed as a primary source of knowledge about man. Failure to recognize that humanity's central concerns have been most faithfully delineated over the centuries by painters, sculptors, and writers is equivalent to renunciation of any real effort to understand the species. Art is an attempt to communicate images, sensations, or ideas from one man to other men, and as such can scarcely avoid being of the essence of human intercourse. It is thus inherently valid as a source of information and suggestion for the student of man. That most pronounced talent of homo sapiens, the ability to conceive of himself and his environment as separable objects of attention, implies that self-searching is the very basis of artistic expression. It is a truism that most first novels are autobiographical; succeeding ones are too, although commonly in lesser degree because the author's widening experience mutes the personal strain. Whence else the insight so vital to creative activity and convincing communication? Introspection is the clue to the first indis-

4

putable value of art as a technique of the social studies. All who analyze human behavior would affirm the proposition that the individual's unique view of life, his own definition of the situation in which he finds himself, is indispensable to the understanding of man singly or men in groups. Artists have obviously provided us with the richest mine of material in existence for the study of self-perception.

Psychology, especially in those aspects committed to deep clinical assessment of the whole personality, is naturally the closest ally and most direct heir of literary techniques. The more fully aware among professional psychologists are quite prepared to admit that literary representations of character have a measure of coherence and a fullness of descriptive detail unapproached by the sketches of contemporary psychology. Novelists and poets must face different criteria than the scientist in the evaluation of their work; they are not dependent on independent empirical verification of their hypotheses, but rather on judgments of the degree to which their work approaches certain implicit models of stylistic grace and emotional exactitude. The reader, or at least sufficient numbers of readers, must testify that the author's work "rings true," but true or false his statements are not susceptible to the kind of demonstration we expect in science. Thus literary character portrayals may be imprecise or even utterly wrong in terms of our best psychological knowledge. Yet it is certain that the writer conveys an internal symmetry of motives and a

5

keen flavor of experience which are unattainable by science alone and are critical to full comprehension of personality.

Murray attests to the value of literary insight:

> A future historian of social science may be surprised to find that, in writing case histories such as are published here, the psychologists of our time show no sign of having been influenced in any way by the twenty-five centuries of literature which have preceded them. The lines of derivation are quite different. Perhaps there is no enlightenment for a clinician in Aristotle, Lucian, Plutarch, Montaigne, Shakespeare, Bayle, Stendhal, Balzac, Dostoevski, Tolstoy, Nietzche, Proust, and others of their stature; but my suspicion persists that the science of man would be carried forward more surely if those of us who undertook to unravel, interpret, and formulate the life histories of normal or abnormal personalities were familiar with the works of the great masters who, assuming that the understanding and portrayal of motives belonged to their special province, directed their acute intelligences to this office.

This view is further elaborated by Allport. After noting the effect of the natural and social sciences on personality study, he contends that the humanities have been perhaps most powerful of all in their influence on psychology:

6

Throughout the ages, of course, this phenomenon of personal individuality has been depicted and explored by the humanities. The more aesthetic philosophers and the more philosophical artists have always made it their special province of interest.

Allport sees certain specific ways in which the literary approach betters that of psychology, especially in charting the course of natural life history through time:

In literature, personality is never regarded, as it sometimes is in psychology, as a series of unrelated actions. Personality is not like a water-skate, darting hither and yon on the surface of a pond, with its several fugitive excursions having no relation to one another. Good literature never makes the mistake of confusing the personality of man with that of a water-skate. Psychology often does.

Literature observes man as he moves through situations, and knits the diverse facets of the personality into a consistent whole. Psychology can learn much from the artist about the analysis of character traits and the perception of lineaments in the vital subjective image of the self. This is not to deny that writers may make personality too coherent, as Dickens, for instance, so often does. Allport concludes that art may indeed be valuable in the study of man:

Personality is not a problem for science nor a problem for art exclusively, but for both to-

7

gether. Each approach has its merits, but both are needed for even an approximately complete study of the infinite richness of personality.

If one accepts the proposition that the arts in general and literature in particular afford a useful entry into the study of personality, it is proper to ask about their further utility in understanding the social context of personality. What can the writer tell us about those patterns of interpersonal relations which constitute human society? Obviously, the habitual and accidental relations of man to man lie at the very heart of the novel as an art form. Dostoevski does more than present a brilliant picture of Raskolnikov's self-destruction; he also describes a place and time, a slice of Russian society, that teach us much about the social organization of nineteenth-century Russia. Similarly, *The Magic Mountain* explores the detailed style of relationships in a minute social compass which approaches a closed system; *Anna Karenina* treats important aspects of Russian social hierarchy as well as the problem of civilized adultery, and *The Grapes of Wrath* deals in part with the necessary arrangements of a viable, if small and transitory, group life. The inevitable distinctions of power and position in mass industrial society, now or in the future, are nowhere more strikingly set forth than in *Brave New World* or Orwell's *Animal Farm*. The artist, then, explains and describes "what life is like" in a variety of settings; in this endeavor, he conveys not only the elements of social intercourse, with an eye for significant

8

detail, but also the mood or tone of the human circumstance. The social scientist may perhaps array details more economically, for some purposes, than the artist, but it is debatable whether his description ever communicates the feel of a social milieu as effectively as the work of the perceptive artistic observer.

Literature, then, is itself a prime repository of knowledge about human behavior. It can also find an exceedingly important place in the disciplines of psychology, sociology, and anthropology through its effectiveness as a medium of illustration. The concepts of science often impress students and the educated lay public as sterile and barren, remote from the colorful immediacy of life. When these concepts are clothed in literary examples, however, their relevance and explanatory power may be immeasurably better understood. Literature's scientific value is of course not merely that of vibrant illustration; the relation between the arts and social sciences is not a one-way street, for an artistic example may bounce back on the scientist, forcing him to revise his abstract model or teasing him on to more subtle perceptions. Most of the great novels can be used to clarify aspects of sociological theory. Dickens, for instance, abounds in detailed accounts of the difficulties involved in working within, or with changing the traditional institutions of society. Recall only the "miasma" of the law as sketched in the masterly beginning of *Bleak House*.

In the analysis of individual psychology, again, novelists and playwrights give us keen glimpses into the unfolding of motives and the nuances of emotional conflict. Poets, above all, lay bare the human loneliness and the subtle, precise accents of the singer's response to a world he may or may not have made. It is perhaps not the sheer accident of a classical education that led Freud to draw on Greek tragedy for his illustrative symbols in the Oedipal theory, or that contrived the term "lesbian" to denote a particular sexual inclination once known on the isle where Sappho cried. Instances of acute perception into psychodynamics are as numerous as great writers or profound books. From the Bible, or the Platonic dialogues, or the ancient wise books of the Orient to the stories and plays of contemporary Western society, artists have marvelously represented the family drama, the themes of love and hate, and the search for a mature concord of desires.

Literature as an Expression of Society and Personality

Literature may be most broadly considered as an extant and vital part of man's culture, of his equipment for viewing the world and his place in it. Like most facets of culture, literature is enmeshed in the curiously circular pattern which underlies the stability of social arrangements. It is at once a product of human beings and an influence upon them. Just as in child development the parents' modes of behavior are learned by the young and in turn propagated, so in artistic activity the creations are received and to some extent re-expressed in the thoughts and lives of the audience. The arts re-

10

flect the individual minds and social environments from which they spring; but they also have a profound effect on the succeeding texture of that environment and on individual styles of life.

Because literature is always closely tied to a specific language, it is perhaps of all the arts most likely to represent the unique features of the society in which it arises. Unlike painting or music, whose mediums are in a certain sense universal, writing is to a great extent inseparable from the particular culture of which it is one expression. Literature mirrors the life of its times, as language does, although the correspondence is seldom direct or transparently valid. Even when the writer expresses themes or values quite different from those espoused by his compatriots, his rootedness in a common linguistic frame implies that he must refer his conceptions, however divergent, to the major premises of his age. Thus if the writer is not upholding an old order or affirming a conventional perception, his new order or original perception is still dynamically related to the values it refutes or extends. Whether its mirror is the stark confrontation of the dressing-table or the distorting image of the amusement park, literature cannot avoid telling us something both important and true about its social surroundings.

In a variety of instances, literature makes important cultural elements explicit with a clarity unattainable by either the participants or more "objective" reporters. It seems that the artist's peculiar capacity for mixing

11

empathic involvement with shrewd detachment lends him a unique perspective on the stiuations he describes. The growing pains of American social and intellectual independence from Europe, and especially from England, are surely nowhere better analyzed than in the novels of Henry James. *Piers Plowman* tells us much about a certain phase of European culture, not only because it portrays a way of life, but because it was in fact a product of that way of life. Although the arts can provide the student of society with an invaluable description of the details embodied in a style of life—dress, manners, speech forms, and so on—they are perhaps most vital in their communication of the general feeling tone of a culture, the implicit assumptions of value and attitude which underlie the surface flow. Literature is a paramount source of insight for the scientist who attempts to formulate the core values of a culture, to characterize its guiding tenets in brief compass.

If one of our pressing needs is, as it seems to be, for a more thorough understanding of the major features of American life, it would be foolhardy to neglect American literature. Emerson, Thoreau, Melville, Henry James and Henry Adams, the "Genteel Tradition," the poets and novelists of the '20's, the Depression, and our own postwar era—all of these, surely, would be central to such an enterprise. An example from another culture might be seen in the way one's sense of Japanese values, as analyzed by Ruth Benedict in *The Chrysanthemum and the Sword,* is enriched by the study of Lady Murasaki's tenth-century *Tale of Genjii.*

The sociologist may draw on the arts for subtle and subjective interpretations of the gross systematic relations which are his chief concern. Family structure, the hierarchical ordering of society, the patterned activities of a community—these may not be fully comprehended without a close look at what they mean to the persons involved. Literature deals with precisely this question of the meaning of social forms as they are perceived through the individual's lens. Fielding's description of eighteenth-century English gentry is more than amusement; no squire ever acted like Squire Western, yet we acquire from *Tom Jones* a flavor which helps us to understand English society of that period. Such data are, to be sure, a part of English history, but they are also directly pertinent to the present shape of English life. Contemporary Britain is in some sense influenced by the fact that country courtyards knew the tilt of a stirrup–cup or the obeisance of a groom. To derive an example from current living habits of that island, the nature poetry of a Shelley or Wordsworth is very certainly relevant to the "rurban" complexion of modern Britain.

Students of society have made the analysis of the "prerequisites" or invariant features of a social system one of their main tasks. Nowhere have these central characteristics of human organization been more spiritedly treated than in the vast utopian literature. From More's *Utopia* to Bellamy's *Looking Backward,* idealistic writers have tried to depict more or less "perfect" systems; from them we gain not only a notion of what has seemed logically desirable to observers at a given time,

13

but also a vivid account of the implications of social rearrangements for personal life. While social ameliora- tion is not the first aim of the scientist, his thinking must be informed by a knowledge of where societal strains are most acute. Here the literature which is popularly termed "sociological" comes into play. For the liter- ature of social protest is more than the fantasies of mal- contents; it may be a true index of tensions, and such tensions may first be made apparent by the sensitive artistic perceiver. The artist's vision may presage change. From *Uncle Tom's Cabin* and the plays of Gorki to the Farrells and Steinbecks, the artist as reformer has rep- resented strain and been himself a symbol. He has some- times helped speed a radical change in administrative or legal policy and hence in society. The Bazarov of *Fathers and Sons* anticipated, perhaps, a portion of that spirit in nineteenth-century Russia which was to cul- minate in the Soviet experiment.

If literature reflects the society of which its author is a member, it also represents the chief elements in the personalities shaped by a particular social context. Ob- viously there is no single "typical" mode of psychological make-up which can stand for all the varieties of person- ality found in a complicated civilization. There are, however, recurrent major themes in individual func- tioning characteristic of most members of a defined social group. The relatively common features of per- sonality engendered by the child-training patterns and reinforced by the main values of a society have often

14

been most strikingly expressed in literature. We thus find clues in the novel, drama, or poem which indicate something about individual character as well as social environment. The youth of classic Russian novels were rarely happy people; one may speculate that national conditions under the Czars were such as to promote, as one element in the personalities of youthful intellectuals, a feeling of frustration and aimlessness. Again, the poetry of Michael Wigglesworth or the religious dicta of Cotton Mather could not fail to impress one with the fact that the overpowering sense of sin preached by the Puritan theocracy was woven closely into the personalities of early New Englanders. Victorian enthusiasm, optimism, and moral rigor are well-depicted in the great English novels of the age; Dickens, Thackeray, Trollope, diverse as they may be, do exhibit in their fiction many of the principal elements of personality in their society. The psychological props of colonialism in the "high noon of Empire" can scarcely be discussed without frequent reference to Kipling's poems.

The author's own personality may of course be interestingly explored through his work, although there are two significant dangers in this effort. The first danger is that the investigator, forgetting the complexity of artistic creation and the writer's ability to assume many guises, may propose a deceptively simple one-to-one correspondence between man and book. The second is that the analyst may see the writer's personality as wholly typical and representative of his nation or social

15

class milieu, whereas artists with their special gifts and special responsibilities are extremely unlikely to be themselves characteristic products of their environment. A perceptive recent exercise in psychological analysis is Erikson's study of George Bernard Shaw through an examination of his autobiographical writings. Rosenzweig has offered a brilliant essay on Henry James's personality. Albrecht justifies his concern with fiction as a source of insight into motivation:

> This study suggests in general that literary works like other manifestations of human behavior fall into definite patterns consistent with the essential nature of the author; that underlying such truisms as "fiction reflects the personality of the writer" are systems of interrelated and complex meanings largely untouched by aesthetic principles and literary classifications; that autobiographies and memoirs, though often misleading in statement and interpretation, can yield to significant psychological and sociological investigation. . .

Literature as an Influence on Society and Personality

One of Oscar Wilde's more thoughtful aphorisms is that "Nature imitates Art more than Art imitates Nature." This is a brilliant over-statement of the truth that human nature, at least, may be importantly affected by artistic experience. Personalities and societies may owe certain facets of their development to the influence

16

of literary works. The individual artist, especially in literature, is of course molded to some extent by the efforts of his predecessors. But on the broader scene of general human development, literature may also be viewed as a primary source of models, of values and attitudes which condition both individual growth and the content of social institutions. Certainly we recognize the influence of literature on the life-lines of outstanding persons in a variety of professions and environments. Autobiographies point again and again to the remembered effect of a great poem or novel; it is probably just to assume that the Battle of Waterloo was won in the classrooms of Eton, where schoolboys had been for generations steeped in the literature of leadership. One may object that only a tiny fraction of any population is exposed to literature with enough intensity to produce a lasting imprint, but this neglects both the peculiar force exercised on their societies by the best-educated minorities and the remarkable phenomenon of "percolation" through the imitation of the talented by those less gifted and the rehearsal of important themes in inferior, derivative artistic products.

A society's common values are reinforced, and sometimes revised, through the medium of art. If the writer restates the accepted values of a group, and does so in an appealing, convincing fashion, his work shores up the existing system. It may confirm the members of the society in their traditional ways of behaving. The steady church-goer finds support for endless Sunday mornings

17

on a hard pew if he is assured by the novelist that such is indeed the pattern of the elect. An elderly spinster may find that her honor was in fact worth saving if some Victorian heroine wins the world by retaining wholesome virginity. It is noteworthy that the Communist countries have put so much emphasis on the ideological tenor which is expected of their literary figures, in the belief that what the writer says is critical to maintaining totalitarian order. Soviet and satellite leaders evidently feel that the arts are central to social life, and deserving of the time and energy required to monitor them.

While it is more difficult to adduce instances of social change which are intimately related to artistic influences, the literature of social protest does have some impact. There are perhaps two quite different ways in which imaginative works shake the organization of society. The first is direct and restricted; it may be exemplified by the supposed impact of Upton Sinclair's *The Jungle* on the regulation of the American meat-packing industry. Beyond this kind of immediate dramatization, so popular in the "proletarian" novel of the 1920's, lies another, more profound conception of the arts as agent of social change. Here the artist does not call attention to some disorder in the surface forms of contemporary life, but rather presents us with a new way of seeing and valuing. If the new perception is accurate, and the language is adequate to express it, then the work may be woven deeply into the unfolding texture of society. Santayana's *Three Philosophical Poets* shows how, each in his own

18

manner, Lucretius, Dante, and Goethe effected perceptual transformations in European culture. In a less grand but more readily demonstrable sense, the dramas of Ibsen and Shaw may be related to changed concepts of law, responsibility, and sexual roles. The classic statement affirms that the door Nora slams in *A Doll's House* was heard all over Europe; even if it was heard by only a few there seems little doubt that Ibsen stimulated fresh thoughts on marital concord.

Literary experience is seldom considered to be an important factor in the individual's life history. We correctly search first for the interpersonal events, especially the events of early childhood, which Freud and others have shown to be critical in character development. Yet modern man lives in a world of words, a world where almost his every act must be related to a symbolic, linguistic environment. In emphasizing face-to-face encounters, the more subtle relation between writer and reader via the printed page is often overlooked. Reading, however, is as surely a part of experience as any other; far from being a substitute for "real life," it is immersed in real life.

Literature, perhaps, affects the individual most keenly in the development of the positive, forward-reaching regions of the self. It helps to set the goals of life-style and character attainment which may be summed up as the ego-ideal, or ideal of self. The maturing individual is known by modern psychology to be capable of change, of directed pursuit of values commensurate with adult life; it is just these sophisticated, often highly conscious shifts in posture which seem most susceptible to literary influence. Artistic experience, says Allport, may seriously determine the path of intellectual and emotional development:

> However entered, if it is entered at all, the world of ideas is a factor that shapes the more complex reaches of personality, and not infrequently it is the most important factor of all.

Examples of literary revelation and inspiration are legion. One might mention Heywood Broun's statement that the reading of *Looking Backward* turned him toward socialism, or the report that China's Mao Tse-Tung greatly admired "heroic" novels at an early age. Literature, since one of its prime goals is character portrayal, naturally abounds in descriptions of social roles. Not only may the reader gain from artistic representations a conception of what is required in his relations with others, what his reactions should be to the actions of other people in their roles, but he may be stimulated in the choice and definition of those of his own roles which are more or less self-determined. An individual does not choose the role of son or daughter, but he does to some extent select the role of father or friend, lover or lawyer. In the former instances, he may model his behavior along lines suggested by fictional characters; in the latter, both desire for the role and patterns through which it is realized may be based in part on literary example. The ego-ideal, the individual's subjective por-

20

trait of the sort of person he would like to be, may in extreme cases be derived directly from some admired character in a novel or play. More often this ideal of self is a composite creation, a blend of favored exemplars in which fictional models are a large element. Allport says in *Personality*:

> Every mature personality may be said to travel toward a port of destination, selected in advance, or to several related ports in succession, the Ego-ideal always serving to hold the course in view.

The ports of this journey, and the means of travel, often owe much to the conscious or unconscious trying out of "parts" first encountered in literature.

Literature should, then, be regarded as a field in which the nature of man may be richly explored. It is at once a part of man's culture—his total fund of styles for living—and a detached commentary on that culture. Resulting from the individuals of a society, it indicates certain things about them and their forms of group behavior. Acting upon the reader, literary works are a shaping force in personality development and social organization. The arts and the artist are central, not peripheral, to any informed cognizance of human motives or actions.

The American Poet as an Illustrative Case

The creative activity and social role of the poet in contemporary America may be seen as special instances

21

of the general framework sketched above. It would obviously be impossible to consider all the relationships implied by this discussion; therefore the poet's mode of work—the actual writing job—and his career in our society will be the chief objects of interest. The account is in many ways incomplete and tentative, most seriously so in its failure to examine American poetry itself, as distinct from its creators, in relation to our current social scene.

In choosing the poet for study, one recognizably weakens the argument for literature as a reflection of society. Poetry is perhaps the least "culture-bound" of literary arts, and its very timelessness is partially based on the possibility of its divorce from specific social milieus. This is especially true of the personal lyric, which deals with universal psychological themes; even here, however, such poems as the ancient Chinese lyrics capture the courts and cities of that distant landscape. Unlike the long descriptive poem or the bulky three-volume novel, modern verse may draw relatively little from the manners of its particular time and place. Yet the *lack* of overt representation, the exclusion of the descriptive elements so marked in, say, epic verse, may be an important clue to the relation between contemporary poetry and the society in which it is written.

American poetry in the middle of the twentieth century assumes a variety of forms; it is by no means standardized, but exhibits instead a flourishing catholicity. Perhaps modern verse is most easily characterized by a

22

negative definition, by attempting to say what it is *not,* rather than what it is. It is not, broadly speaking, conceived in the epic mold; the culture is not summed up through dramatic exploits of larger-than-life heroes, as in the antique Greek and Norse sagas. The poet does not ordinarily describe events and surroundings in narrative form, nor does he explicitly toy with the customs and conceits of polite intercourse in the style of Pope. He refrains from preaching or lecturing to his reader, except in the most indirect fashion. What he does do, and consummately well, is exalt and explore the individual consciousness. The world of nature and the world of men are transmuted through his perceptions into their most meaningful forms for the solitary person. The poet, of course, has ever done so; his task is to report subjective responses to the environment, taking environment in its fullest sense to include his inner psychological climate as well as the objective world "out there." What is perhaps singular is the nearly exclusive emphasis on this highly personal mode, to the neglect of the story-telling and reporting which once supplemented the concern with individual psychic verities.

If, from a traditional store of literary styles, an age selects those forms—the lyric cry, the tautly introspective analysis, the philosophical-psychological monologue—which magnify the contours of the unique personality, what may be deduced about that age? Perhaps it is not too much to say that one prominent feature of contemporary America is a frantic groping for personal invul-

23

nerability in the face of an increasingly insecure and complicated social environment. The sense of confusion and instability, of ambiguous values and goals, which are so well revealed in the popular thirst for self-help and psychological ease, can scarcely be without effect on poetry. The poet, less able to synthesize his experience in the broad social context, may be driven to a more exclusive synthesis in terms of his unique emotions and highly personal perspectives. He searches for the self rather than enunciating a common core of traditional value. Herbert Read notes that a pre-modern poet, Robert Browning, defined the subjective poet as one who "digs where he stands." The contemporary focus on self-examination in the arts is further expressed by Read in his statement that the modern poet writes "with the knowledge that the truth as he sees it is a private reality of his own."

It is quite true that the "cult of personality" has historical roots, that individual florescence has been an ideal in many times and places, and especially in the Western world since the Renaissance. But the modern fascination with the integrity and health of the solitary ego is acute, perhaps pathological. This obsession with the private world seems directly related to the profusion of alternative values in modern life, the absence of religious and moral consensus, and the increasing invasion of individual discretion by massive social forms as expressed in the media of communication and the organization of work. What some observers would discern as the proper

24

relation between the individual as artist and his social environment has been radically disturbed. These observers, primarily literary critics, are at pains to analyze the disturbance although they seldom provide a positive account of the relation as it ought to be. A typical summary is given by Stallman:

> There is one basic theme in modern criticism; it is the dissociation of modern sensibility. The loss of a spiritual order and of integrity in the modern consciousness is T. S. Eliot's major premise.

> It is a commonplace of criticism—that our present-day world is in radical disintegration and that the artist is severed from a living relation to society.

Yet it would be sensible to avoid a simple equation in which the poet's stress on internal states and idiosyncratic themes is set forth as a reflection of social disorder. The equation has its bit of truth, but it overlooks the integrative aspects of American society, our belief in plural values as opposed to monolithic prescriptions, and our very real underlying "agreements to disagree." It also overlooks the historical *literary* bases of literary behavior: Baudelaire and Rimbaud were never faced with assembly lines, granite canyons, or twentieth-century bureaucracy; yet the modern American poet probably owes as much to French symbolism as to the Manhattan skyline. And not all poets thrive on the stream of consciousness or introspective quest; in the United States

25

we have Robert Hillyer composing traditional sonnets and Carl Sandburg exalting the sinews of Chicago.

The Language of Poetry

The poetry of a people takes its life from the people's speech and in turn gives life to it; and represents its highest point of consciousness, its greatest power and its most delicate sensibility.
—T. S. Eliot

A poet is, before anything else, a person who is passionately in love with language.
—W. H. Auden

THE CORE OF POETRY is language. Unless the poet's language is understood and distinguished from journalistic prose or the tongues of science or politics, one may not only misread the poet but also fail to comprehend the task he is attempting and the specific nature of his relation to society.

As so many poets and critics have affirmed, the poet is distinguished by an exquisite sensitivity to the meanings and music of words. His concern with language is both more intense and more playful than that of the average speaker or writer. This is because so much more of his life, of his total personality, is involved in the verbal world. And his meaning is always multiple, as life is always multiple; ambiguity is not only often deliberately contrived, but is an inevitable consequence of the fact that life, like language, proceeds on many levels and tangents. The clarity of a highway sign or a scientific formula indicates that a single restricted aspect of reality is in question. The clarity or lack of it in a poem indicates that a total experience is in question.

The language of poetry is an important part of man's recorded history. What we know of pre-history and primitive groups would testify that as spoken tradition it is also central in his unrecorded history. Thus poetic expression comes to represent or sum up human activity for succeeding eras as well as for the poet's contemporaries. When Kroeber set out to study patterns of cultural growth, he fixed on literature as one vehicle through which growth might be traced. His choice is illuminating because it demonstrates the dependence of a gifted anthropologist, a scholar interested in the analysis of man's total behavior, on the intrinsic significance of artistic behavior. For his broad survey, Kroeber needed manifestations which were relatively independent of particular human agents or unique historical settings, and which were readily available. The arts met these criteria because their language is in a certain sense autonomous and because they have been valued and saved through the centuries. Art lasts; it has been prized in most times and places, even when its creators have been

28

inadequately rewarded in the days of their working. In company with philosophy, religion, and the sciences, the arts may be seen as the enduring precipitates of human society.

An inquiry into the way in which poetry communicates ideas, emotions, and images from one person to another is thus essential to the analysis of creativity and the social role of the creative individual. Poetry is not an occult tongue, but a language firmly grounded in the basic design of human relations, of individuals in face-to-face communion. Although the poet today is a highly specialized and accomplished craftsman, and his work tends to be read silently rather than voiced, most poets would affirm that the intent and style of verse implies the human breath and vocal capacity. The lyric cry is the lover's cry, and love is not made at a distance. The poet tells of things heard and seen and felt; at root the process is not different from the intimate congress in which two or more people make things clear to themselves and to one another by the exchange of word and gesture. The written poem is only a facility for further clarifying the poet's intent to himself through internal dialogue; for reaching more hearers than are present at the time of writing; and for preserving the expression to the benefit of absent listeners and those unborn.

The poem is a striking example of the way aesthetic forms may arise in social intercourse and then develop into sophisticated patterns of written tradition. Most observers place the origin of poetry in face-to-face recitals

29

of events, often bound up with song and rhythm. In its earliest form, poetry seems to have been a medium of communication at the group level; the chants and choruses were more like community anthems than expressions of one individual's—the poet's—unique view. Herbert Read emphasizes that early poetry, crystallized in the ballad form, was marked by simplicity and rhythm which appealed to the whole social group. Gummere called "the cadence of consenting feet" the first cause of poetry.

An exceedingly interesting and cogent account of poetic development, based on the premise that the arts are born of the human talent for play, is given by Johan Huizinga. He charts the great instances of epic verse as a demonstration that poetry arises in verbal games, contests of story-telling in which the participants vie for command through the compelling magic of words: "The creative function we call poetry is rooted in a function even more primordial than culture itself, namely play." And again, "To call poetry, as Paul Valéry has done, a playing with words and language is no metaphor: it is the precise and literal truth." Huizinga describes the language of poetry as a primary medium for conveying the paramount concerns of a society, and the poet as historically a social leader:

> Civilization is always slow to abandon the verse form as the chief means of expressing things of importance to the life of the community. Poetry everywhere precedes prose; for

30

the utterance of solemn or holy things poetry is
the only adequate vessel.

In Germanic law, certain key provisions were defined
in verse. And "up to 1868 the Japanese used to compose
the weightiest part of a State document in poetic form."

Finally, speaking of the early Greek poets, Huizinga
recalls:

Their function is eminently a social one; they
speak as the educators and monitors of their
people. They are the nation's leaders, whose
place was later usurped by the sophists.

If poetic discourse has been a characteristic human
activity, and its results have been socially valued, how
may its nature be described and its import be distinguished from the import of other languages which serve
different ends? Man has often been termed the symbol-
using animal, the elaborator of a universe in which objects and experiences can be conceived apart from their
immediate situation, their direct impact on the perceiver. Suzanne Langer assumes that human beings have
a "need to symbolize;" whether or not such a need can be
identified as an innate property of the organism, it is
certain that the child rapidly develops a thirst for symbolic activity as an inevitable part of growth. The world
into which he is initiated is in very large measure one
of words, and is organized for him by the system of
language in which he matures.

Langer makes an important distinction between two
types of symbolism; while one might argue that the two

31

could be refined into several more types, the primary
division is clear. She speaks of "discursive" and "presentational" symbolism. The "discursive" mode is the one
most familiar to us: it is the language of the more deliberate, rational phases of mundane affairs and also of the
greater part of scholarship and the sciences. It is the
prototype of logical, cognitive "pointing" to known or
assumed entities, an explicit reference to one thing at a
time in which the user's meaning is ideally single and
unmistakable. Such language explains or abstracts from
experience for certain definite purposes and has an end-
in-view beyond itself; the words are in one sense "un-
important," serving as an instrument for something else.
It is commonly redundant in high degree, because the
message must be communicated with many qualifications
and repetitions in order to insure a minimum of ambiguity.

The "presentational" type of symbolism is more difficult to define, since it does not always serve an obvious
end, does not necessarily facilitate action toward some
readily discernible goal. Rather, it conveys a general
sense of experience in a way that is immediately gratifying and valued for its own sake. In Langer's words:

> Art . . . has no consequences; it gives form to
> something that is simply there, as the intuitive
> organizing functions of sense give form to ob-
> jects and spaces, color and sound.

> To understand the "idea" in a work of art is
> therefore more like *having a new experience*

than like entertaining a new proposition.

Langer fashions her new key for philosophy out of the recognition that presentational symbols, of which the arts are an exemplar, are crucial to understanding men in society. She believes this language to be equally as important as the other major variety of "strictly referential" language. Her thesis portends the growing interest in aesthetic experience in the modern West, the feeling that our scientific "mapping" falls short of adequate knowledge if it fails to consider these elements of life.

The language of poetry then contrives to present an immediacy of experience, so that perceiving a poem is itself a pleasant and valuable activity. But the activity obviously does not cease when the poet's voice is stilled or the reader closes his book. If deeply perceived, the poem may be expected to go on working, to inform the subsequent life of the reader in one or several ways. Perhaps the most general statement of the poem's ideal effect is that it enhances the reader's own capacity for experience and sharpens his consciousness of the nuances in his relationship to himself and others. Poetic language has been credited too with the capacity to inspire belief and order an individual's total philosophy or worldview. While some purists in philosophy and criticism would insist literally on Langer's dictum that "art has no consequences," many observers have attributed it persuasive power. Ernst Cassirer and others have stressed the cognitive element in myth. Psychoanalysis and anthropology affirm that the arts are related both to the patterns of individual psychological development and to the genesis of group tradition. The symbols of poetry recall to us significant ways of viewing the world, ancient ideals, conflicts, resolutions. Maud Bodkin maintains that poetry is religious experience, that it means to her what she assumes is the essential character of religion. She cites Santayana's conclusion that poetry is "religion without points of application in conduct, and without an expression in worship and dogma," and that "our religion is the poetry in which we believe."

One of poetry's most significant effects on society, and one assumed by many poets to be paramount, is the invention and refreshment of language. Although it is proper to consider poetry as a particular kind of discourse, it is equally important to realize that the poet's tongue affects linguistic custom in general and that his special language is part of language-as-a-whole. The poet is generically a language-maker in his struggle to express experience in the most complete manner. As a professional perceiver he constantly strains language to the breaking point, for language becomes worn and used, common and conventional, and thus ill-fitting to the fresh view. The poet's effort to "say what he means" is a source of new words and a force for renewing and enriching the old. Thus linguistic facility on the poet's part results in a net gain to the linguistic fund of society. Otto Rank evolves his entire theory of the creative process in art from a consideration of the poet as user of language, and Emerson moves the poet onstage when

34

"the world is put under the mind for verb and noun."

Finally, Charles Morris, speaking of poetry as a basic type of human communication, emphasizes how intimately it is concerned with the values men practice or envision:

> The great significance of poetic discourse lies in the vivid and direct way that it records and sustains achieved valuations, and explores and strengthens novel valuations.

> Poetry then not merely records what in fact men have found significant, but plays a dynamic role in the development and integration of valuative attitudes and explicit valuations. Poetry at its best is a symbolic antenna of behavior at the immediate frontier of its valuational creativity.

The problem of distinguishing poetry from other types of language is one of the most vexed in the history of philosophy, criticism, and semantics. One difficulty is undoubtedly the fact that language is an organic, living thing, that poetry, like experience, does not lend itself to easy description or fit neatly into categories. Perhaps the task of discriminating aesthetic symbolism may be best approached through consideration of a very old controversy, that between poetry and science, or between empirically verifiable statements and humanly felt-to-be-true expressions which do not adhere to formal criteria of evidence.

The great debate on varieties of symbolism was initiated for our times by Ogden and Richards in *The Meaning of Meaning*. They separated what they termed "symbolic" use of language from "evocative" use. Symbolic language aims at the precise transmission of information, while evocative language has the goal of arousing attitudes in an emotional setting. Symbolic usage is "referential," in that we can isolate objects or ideas to which it explicitly refers. Evocative usage is "emotive," in that it does not convey knowledge or specific referents but provides a general emotional stimulus. The refinement of this initial distinction has proceeded mainly by revealing the logic and information carried by aesthetic experience[1] and by protesting against so simple a separation. Pollack has protested, too, that Ogden and Richards tend to exaggerate the importance of scientific, logical language and thus assign literature to a residual place in the total linguistic scheme; poetry is "left over" after the primary function of language—the unambiguous transmission of logical statements—has been accounted for. Richards goes on later, in *Science and Poetry,* to argue that poetry deals with "pseudo-statements": "The acceptance which a pseudo-statement receives is entirely governed by its effects upon our feelings and attitudes." Although Richards is a defender, not to say an apostle,

---

[1] See, for instance, Max Black's paper in "A Symposium on Emotive Meaning," *The Philosophical Review,* March, 1948.

of poetry, his theory of language seems to divorce poetry from other modes of discourse to the implicit intellectual detriment of poetic language.

Lewis also distinguishes two major aspects of language, which he calls the cognitive and the "orectic." Orectic language, which includes poetry, is oriented to values and emotional responses rather than to verifiable knowledge. One of his important insights is that poetic language comes earliest in the child's life, and is then constantly trained out of the socially conforming person by the exclusive stress on cognitive language in most phases of education. He thus points up the possibility that men in modern society are weaned away from involvement and intuitive familiarity with expressive symbolism. This incapacity is seen as a fundamental problem in highly sophisticated societies, because although poetry and other aesthetic forms, as well as the ready gestures of face-to-face relations, continue to be of great significance, men have lost their awareness and mastery of language which is not directed to a useful demonstrable purpose.

Such a contention echoes Langer's concern and further justifies a renewed attention to aesthetic symbolism. Our faith in unaided reason has been shaken by Freud, surely the most rational of men; our faith in science has been shaken by atomic rehearsals and the notable failure of technological virtuosity to guarantee happy comfort. Perhaps the impact of Freud's thought has been most critically felt as a recalling to consideration of those ele-

ments in human existence which resist thorough understanding and systematic appraisal. The limits of scientific
knowledge as proclaimed by scientists themselves,
and the recognition that at its frontier science embraces
poetic intuition (Robert Oppenheimer's voice is in large
measure the poet's voice) compel us to search for the
significance of poetic language. And the search is patently more than an exercise in logic or semantics: it is
a quest for understanding the full human experience.

An unusually perceptive account of the differences
between literature and other forms of symbolism is given
by Pollack. He proposes that science may be thought of
as communicating the results of an experience or pointing to an experience, while literature conveys the essential
quality of the experience itself. The drift of his argument confirms both Langer and Morris in their realization of the immediate and self-contained nature of art.
Morris has called the "self-reference" of the aesthetic
symbol its *iconic* property; it does not "point" to something else but itself embodies the creator's intent. It is
important to note that the distinction is not really
between abstract and immediate means but between
abstract and immediate ends. Although science and
poetry both must abstract from the total flux of life,
science points toward a specific aspect of experience for
a certain further purpose while poetry tries to recreate
the poet's experience in the reader for the sake of the
experience itself. The idea that abstraction is as relevant
to poetry as to other languages is well stated in T. S.

38

Eliot's "objective correlative": "a set of objects, a situation, a chain of events which shall be the formula of that particular emotion; such that when the external facts, which must terminate in sensory experience, are given, the emotion is immediately evoked." The notion of art as experience must then be refined, and its immediacy must be viewed as a link between the state of the creator and the state of the appreciator.

Perhaps the essence of the poetic symbol may finally be best understood poetically. The language of poetry resists analysis, and one of its distinguishing features is precisely the fact that it cannot be adequately translated into expository prose. The most penetrating elucidation of a metaphor never quite succeeds in undercutting it. Among several intriguing efforts by modern poets to define the art in verse, the two following seem especially pertinent:

A poem should be palpable and mute
as a globed fruit

Dumb
As old medallions to the thumb

Silent as the sleeve-worn stone
Of casement ledges where the moss has grown—

A poem should be wordless
As the flight of birds

A poem should be motionless in time
As the moon climbs

Leaving, as the moon releases
Twig by twig the night-entangled trees,

Leaving, as the moon behind the winter leaves,
Memory by memory the mind—

A poem should be motionless in time
As the moon climbs

A poem should be equal to:
Not true

For all the history of grief
An empty doorway and a maple leaf

For love
The leaning grasses and two lights above the sea—

A poem should not mean
But be.

—Archibald MacLeish, "Ars Poetica"

I, too, dislike it: there are things that are important
beyond all this fiddle.
Reading it, however, with a perfect contempt for it,
one discovers in it after all, a place for the genuine
Hands that can grasp, eyes
that can dilate, hair that can rise
if it must, these things are important not
because a
high-sounding interpretation can be put upon them but
because they are useful. When they become so derivative as to become unintelligible, the same thing

40

may be said for all of us, that we
do not admire what
we cannot understand: the bat
holding on upside down or in quest of
something to
eat, elephants pushing, a wild horse taking a roll, a tire-
less wolf under a tree, the immovable critic twitch-
ing his skin like a horse that
feels a flea, the base-
ball fan, the statistician—
nor is it valid
to discriminate against 'business documents
and
school-books'; all these phenomena are important. One
must make a distinction however: when dragged
into prominence by half poets,
the result is not poetry,
nor till the poets among us can be
'literalists of
the imagination'—above
insolence and triviality and can present
for inspection, imaginary gardens with real toads in
them, shall we have it. In the meantime, if you demand on the one hand, the raw material of poetry in
all its rawness and
that which is on the other hand
genuine, then you are interested in poetry.

—Marianne Moore, "Poetry"

41

At least two themes in these poems are directly relevant to the effort to define poetic language. MacLeish's well-known conclusion that "a poem should not mean but be" indicates again the difference between the logical pointing of science and the total emotional representation of art. Marianne Moore's insistence on the "genuine" quality of poetry, on the poet as "literalist of the imagination," emphasizes the fact that poetry is not a disembodied fantasy; not at all remote from the "real world," poetry is a scrupulous report, a precision-ground lens through which we view the exact truth of the poet's perception.

The arduous job of capturing experience in words is likely to involve the poet in various sorts of personal strain. The use of highly sophisticated symbols, particularly those representing emotional states, has sometimes been seen as damaging to psychological health. The world of words is, biologically speaking, quite artificial. Without special reference to aesthetic symbols Burrow proposes that the fore-brain in man, site of his capacity to manipulate symbols, is also the locus of his neurotic difficulties. Men are prone to a kind of dislocation in which their virtuosity in the use of symbols outstrips their cohesion as biological organisms. The dislocation, Burrows feels, is rooted in man's tendency to "project," or read into situations things which are not objectively present in the outer world of objects and persons but exist only in the individual's imagination. His cure would apparently be a state of stolid grace in which tension had been ruled out by perfect integration of organic condition and symbolic activity. But this resolution of the strains forced on the individual by his symbol-using talent seems to leave little room for the positive aspects; just as the gulf between symbolism and physiology may be man's tragic dualism, so it may be his greatest glory. For what are the great works of art but projective responses to life?

One careful student of language finds that emotionally intense symbols accompany emotional "disturbance." Zipf states that emotional intensity in language is found where the personality is in a condition of change, "a breach in the established patterns of behavior." Since nature desires a re-balancing of the pattern which has been breached, emotional experiences are translated into prosaic language as a critical step in the individual's return to stable behavior. Therefore we might conclude that the creator, and in some cases the very acute appreciator, of poetic symbols is exposed to strain; novel aesthetic experience obviously does shake the comfortable habits of daily life. Extended awareness of one's emotional states may become pathological since it involves the recognition of inconsistencies and irreconcilable themes in the personality—or in life itself. Although it must be conceded that self-exploration is a hazardous enterprise, poets and those sensitive to their tongue would probably maintain that the game is worth the candle: perceived truth and beauty are valuable even at the cost of psychic ease, and heightened consciousness may lead the individual to a new level of personal fulfillment.

Poetic language is then to be distinguished from other language, but the distinguishing criteria cannot be grounded in a "competition" of symbolic usage. As Richards stresses, the acrimony between poetry and science is usually based on a misunderstanding of poetry, an assumption that the poet is telling us something by means of strictly logical reference. In a very real sense, we have forgotten how to respond to the poet's language, how to accommodate symbols which represent experience but do not always explicitly point or explain. Poetry, science, and other discourses have each a legitimate function. The nature of language and of behavior indicates that the various symbolic modes cannot usurp one another's province. All symbolism abstracts from the full reality of man-in-time, since that reality is too multifarious to be adequately represented. But different modes abstract for different purposes. The variability of experience implies a congeries of possible perceptions, and these perceptions are independently valid depending on the specific criteria of validity which one chooses to invoke.

Aesthetic symbolism aims at a recreation of experience. The creator's perception is to be renewed and evoked for his audience by the stimulus of these symbols. The fuller the response, presumably, the better. Poetry embraces ambiguity; the poet is not dismayed if his work arouses varieties of experience. Other symbolism, of

44

which science and logic are typical, aims at the elucidation of strictly defined referents and the relations among them. And the scientist *is* shocked if the language he employs does not cue the reader to exact recognition of the entities to which he is "strictly referring." Science has its jargon because it must fix precise labels on the things with which it deals, and its meanings must be unmistakable. Poetry has its music because it is concerned with presenting a total mood, with *being* something rather than *pointing to* something. As Morris has concisely stated:

> Only the individual who utilizes the signs of the artists, the prophets, and the philosophers, as well as the information given to him by the scientists, is living at the level of a complex individual.

It would probably be protested by many American readers that Morris's counsel to heed the poet's signs is an impractical advice. The well-known "difficulty" of modern verse tends to insure that our poets are unread even when they are most admired. While this is not the place for critical exegesis, some few aspects of the failure to communicate must be considered if we are to understand the poet's creative work or his general status in American society. One of the most important features is a failure on the part of readers, not of poets, to attend to poetic language. Part of the disinclination to read poetry, or if reading it to be in any way deeply affected, undoubtedly may be traced to modern culture's empha-

45

sis upon the language of cognitive pointing. We are not habituated to symbols as the carriers of general emotional experience, but rather as signposts to digested information. But our aesthetic incapacity cannot be attributed wholly to the society's ardor for "facts" or its marriage to an impoverished utilitarian quest for immediate practical efficacy. A spiritual indolence must also be remarked in our preference for quiz shows and the comforting prose of the Sunday supplement; as Randall Jarrell and others have pointed out, the poetry of past ages is by no means easy reading. Some effort has always been required to apprehend the poet's meaning. Poetry demands a close reading and an energetic willingness to suspend the disbelief which we always feel in the presence of a fresh perception or a revolutionary judgment.

Since poetry is an interpersonal process, the other party to the relationship—the poet himself—must also bear responsibility for the blocking of his message. He speaks, it is often complained, in a private language burdened with symbols which mean much to the poet but very little to a reader who is not privy to the unique code employed. Erich Heller dates the "hazard" of poetry, its character as a special language, from the triumph of the scientific spirit at the close of the Middle Ages. When religious and artistic symbols became "merely" symbols, divorced from what was termed the "real" world of sensory fact, the poet turned inward in self-conscious alienation from his environment:

For ambiguity and paradox are the manner

46

of speaking when reality and symbol, man's
mind and his soul, are at cross-purposes.

The notorious obscurity of modern poetry is
due to the absence from our lives of commonly
accepted symbols to represent and house our
deepest feelings.

Thus it is possible to come full circle and fix the
incapacity of both poet and reader in their shared cultural climate. If the language of poetry has often become
too exotic for congenial discourse, however, it has continued to develop as a vehicle for the poet's exploration
of self. This development implies that the exploration
has gone forward, and that our age of self-analysis may
once again be able to accept the poet as a guide. We
may in fact find the poet's tongue animating more
people, or at any rate inspiring them in their own search
for selfhood. In one sense the poet's voyage to a private
world has become the common pilgrimage; and it must
never be forgotten that he sends back a signal from his
voyage, even if it sometimes sounds feebly on our numbed
ears.

Heller summarizes the history of recent poetry:

But what is to happen if doubt about the
true stature of things invades the very sphere of
experience and intuitive insight in which poetry
is formed? If suspicion attacks the value of the
real world? Then the poetic impulse will seek
refuge in a sphere all its own, a little cosmos
of inwardness salvaged from the devaluation of

47

the world. "The Discovery and Colonisation of
Inwardness"—this might be a fitting title for
the story of poetry from the Renaissance to our
day.

The "Colonisation of Inwardness" proceeds by an
attempt to fathom one's response to experience, to sound
the depths of the self with great precision. The attempt,
occurring in words, is highly individual; but it is also
highly social, since despite all the obstacles we have re-
hearsed the poet draws primarily on a common fund of
language and communication does take place.

Creativity—The Self as Vocation

> Above all, the writing of a poem brings one face to face with his own personality with all its familiar and clumsy limitations. In every other phase of existence, one can exercise the orthodoxy of a conventional routine: one can be polite to one's friends, one can get through the day at the office, one can pose, one can draw attention to one's position in society, one is— in a word—dealing with men. In poetry, one is wrestling with a god."
>
> —Stephen Spender

THE POET'S WORK is based on an exhaustive use of his own personality. If his means are his stock of words and facility in shaping them to artistic form, his ends are to transmute experience through his own view of life, his unique perceptual stance. Thus both instruments and goals of the poetic task center around the qualities and capacities of the self. The self is truly a vocation for the creative artist, in a way that seems unlike that of the individual in any other type of activity. Psychologically, then, the poet is man made plain because no other man explores the self so relentlessly or exhibits it so beautifully. In Emerson's words, "He stands among partial men for the complete man, and apprises us not of his wealth, but of the common wealth."

There have been many theories of creativity in the arts, and the relation of the creative act to the artist's personality. No single explanation satisfies all the vagaries of creative work, perhaps because that work is itself fundamentally mysterious even to those who perform it. The creative process resists analysis by its very nature; if the whole scheme could be neatly blocked out, it would lose the novelty and freshness which is its distinguishing characteristic. Yet the poet's central job is the writing of a poem, and any discussion of his role must begin with this act. While the exploration will draw on the ideas of philosophers and psychologists, our primary evidence must be the reports of poets themselves, especially the modern American poets.

The cardinal assumption about literary creativity on which this discussion rests is that the *process* of writing and the *personality* of the writer are parts of the same whole. Since there are many sorts of people who write poetry, their most obvious common feature is the involvement in the poet's craft. To say that *only* persons who have a special psychological make-up are capable of creative writing is a crude simplification; it leads to the "nothing-but—" fallacy in which complicated patterns of talent and effort are dismissed with a nod toward

Oedipus or some other psychoanalytic slogan. Moreover, it seems wiser to start with something on which a good deal of testimony is available—the process of writing—than with the vague impressions of partisan observers who regard all writers as paragons or emotional cripples.

The Poetic Process

One violates reality when he splits the poet's vocation into separate compartments. It is arbitrary and artificial to divide creativity into sections. Yet a study of chronological stages may help in gripping this very slippery process. There is too an obvious progression involved, from blank page to finished poem, although it seldom occurs in a straight line without much backtracking and crisscrossing. A rough model of the phases of poetic creativity would include at least these elements: selective perception of the environment; acquisition of technique; envisioning of combinations and distillations; elucidation of the vision; and the end of the poem and its meaning to the poet. Each of the elements should be examined in some detail.

Selective Perception of the Environment

From the moment of birth the person is exposed to a multitude of stimuli. These may be mainly physical at the start, but are soon overlain with emotional experiences in great variety. Accompanying the emotional learning involved in the relation to the mother and other significant figures is a learning of bodily motions

51

and of the relations among objects. The child in due
course discovers himself, realizes his individuality and
identity, and perceives relations between this self and
external entities. All experience accumulates to form a
store of impressions, images, and ideas—the self upon
which later excursions in life, artistic and otherwise, are
founded. The particular combinations of stimuli are
unique; but at the same time individuals in a given
society partake of a common fund of greater or lesser
extent. From the first fact stems the inherent individuality of the human being, and his capacity for creating
something utterly personal; from the second, the insurance that what he creates will have sufficient social
relevance to be minimally communicable. The total fund
of experience is the "well" of J. L. Lowes, the source of
material for creative effort. At this point it is unnecessary to distinguish subportions of this experience; certainly it is a store whose stock includes sensory
impressions and a variety of mental content, both conscious and unconscious. Psychoanalytic knowledge would
certify that it is always more extensive than the person
can consciously "realize" at any point in time. The
acquisition of experience is variable in both extensity and
intensity. It is probable that the artist registers more
experience than the noncreative person, but it is more
certain, and more important, that he registers experience
with greater intensity. The qualitative difference in intake between creator and non-creator may be subsumed
under the overworked concept of sensitivity. It is a cri-

terion of the artist that he is more *aware* than others, more permeable to the impressions of outer and inner stimuli.[1] However, we must note that the highly aware person is not guaranteed creative gifts, that sensitivity is a precondition but not an assurance of creativity. An extremely sensitive person may never learn how to use art forms or have the energy necessary to disciplined expressive action. Further, the sensitivity which facilitates rich experiencing must, in the case of the artist, sooner or later be allied to a discriminating function, so that experience is weighted according to some value scale. This scale is implicit, but must be present if one is to distinguish the artist from an amorphous sponge soaking up everything in sight regardless of worth.

Four major sources of stimuli may be proposed as essential in the development of the poet's fund of experience: the gross natural environment, interpersonal relations, symbol systems, and the self.

The *gross natural environment* would include the world of nature and human artifacts which do not constitute a recognized symbol system. Much of the imagery on which the word-artist depends has roots in

---

[1] This point has been brought emphatically to my attention by Conrad Aiken, who makes increasing awareness the key to his philosophy of artistic activity.

nature—process and object—and in inanimate things.[2]

As to *interpersonal relations,* the artist grows and lives in an atmosphere of human interaction. From his immediate mentors in the family comes the capacity for love and identification. Emotional responses are learned, and the techniques of empathy are nurtured. Interpersonal relations are the focus for the person's learning to take the attitude of the other, and to be fully himself. This order of experience is critical to future expressive activity, and especially to creative work; it implies that the artist can learn to judge motivations accurately, and transmit his art to others in such a form that they can recognize its validity in human terms.

One *symbol system*—language—underlies all poetic actions. Language is the mold for the bulk of the person's experience, and the form into which his impressions of all kinds must be translated for communication. Fortunately much of the translation takes place almost immediately on the reception of stimuli, so that what is later recalled is already in symbolic linguistic form.[3] The

---

[2] James Laughlin entitles a book of his poems, *Some Natural Things* (Norfolk, Conn.: New Directions, 1945), and has indicated in conversation that natural objects provide the main instigation for his creative efforts.

[3] Karl Shapiro has emphasized that the predominance of the verbal is in him so acute that sense impressions must usually undergo an immediate transformation into words if they are to be fully meaningful.

word-artist is usually a person infatuated with language, ultra-sensitive to its shadings and differential impacts, and to precision in its use.

Theodore Spencer gives poetic point to the verbal artist's concern with language in his "Reason for Writing."

> No word that is not flesh, he said,
> Can hold my wavering ear; but when
> That golden physical flesh is clear,
> *I dance in a glory like your glory*
> *With force to stir the dead.*
>
> No word that is not thought, he said,
> Can hook my slippery mind; but when
> That silver accurate thought I find,
> *I dance in a glory like your glory*
> *With force to stir the dead.*
>
> Words both flesh and thought, he said,
> Hold and hook my heart; and when
> The gold, the silver, shudder apart,
> *Still in a glory like your glory*
> *I'll dance to stir the dead.*

Language becomes for us all the mirror of the world; most of us use it with a fairly low level of alertness, but it is the peculiar virtue of the literary artist to employ words with a maximum awareness of their special qualities. It has been suggested that the cultural pressure of conventional language forces the child to accept stereotyped ways of seeing and thinking, and that conformity is therefore built in by the inexorable demands of a common language. According to this view held by Schachtel, the creative person would be one who in fact rejects the conventions of word usage in favor of a more perceptive concentration upon exact meanings, one who can retain the capacity for seeing as the child supposedly sees, in complete freshness and wonder. There is considerable support for this notion in the emphasis placed by artists upon the maintenance of curiosity, of the gift of wonder. It would seem that the truth of this conception is valid but partial—that the artist must indeed reserve the facility to see anew each day and to be unfettered by the deadening force of trite expressive mechanisms, but that he must to some degree accept linguistic convention if communication is to occur. Moreover, although one may inveigh against the restraints of ordinary usage, it is obvious that the child must receive the cultural imperatives of a philosophy-in-language[4] before he can go on to refine, reject, and revivify that philosophy. Unless he first accepts the con-

---

[4] One of the great insights of the developing study of semantics is an appreciation of the extent to which language embodies in its very structure the cultural way-of-seeing of its primary users. See especially B. L. Whorf, *Four Articles on Metalinguistics* (Washington, D. C.: Foreign Service Institute, 1950); and D. D. Lee, "A Primitive System of Values," *Philosophy of Science,* (1940), VII:355-378.

ventions of his own tongue, the artist would be without the equipment for social life itself, to say nothing of creative effort. Thus, he must both accept and discriminate in his linguistic intake. A civilized being must be nurtured in *some* culture, accept *some* predetermined ways of seeing; otherwise, one would expect feral children to be the world's greatest literary artists. Creativity does not occur in a vacuum.

Literature itself is one of the poet's most important sources of experience. The environment which is perceived and sensitively amassed as the basis of creativity includes the heritage of past creators. The primitive is a rarity even in painting, and is in verbal creativity almost unknown. The tradition of the art form to be pursued is as much an essential element of the experiential well as the images of natural objects themselves. There are few literary artists of today who would be subject to Dr. Johnson's criticism of the playwright who had written more than he had read. The individual must work within a culture even if he is bent on eventually transcending certain portions of that culture. The poet not only masters the forms of his art, but also accumulates philosophical, historical, religious and even scientific knowledge which in some instances matches that of the professional scholar.

The self is a part of its own environment. Perception of the self by the self forms a significant component of experience. It is a truism that the creative artist uses himself—that is, employs his own experience, seen as

57

object, in his expressive effort. The picture of the self
which the person infers and constructs in his introspective maneuvers is the artist's prime source of material
and knowledge. It is the basic insurance that his moti-
vational insights will be accurate, and is the first testing
ground for the validity of his conceptions. This is so
despite the fact that the person may introspect in "error"
as gauged by certain objective standards; what he sees
within is true for him and is his last resort as creator.
The meaning of great art work for large numbers of
people, and through many generations, attests that the
single creator's self-examination is not infinitely dis-
torted. If it were, there would be no communication by
means of art and no standards of esthetic value and
relevance. As science in the last analysis rests upon the
consensus of informed observers, so verbal art survives
through an implicit agreement in the hearts and minds
of men that what the artist has said is "true"—at least
for them. The poet explores the self, and thus the self
that is tapped must be a richer, fuller whole in him than
in other men if his work is to be finally significant and
relevant to the general human enterprise.

The Acquisition of Technique

The richest and most varied experience leads to no
poem unless it is translated into recognizable poetic
form. Eliot somewhere remarks that the sign of distinction in a young poet is not the content of his work,
which is likely to be trite, but the way in which it is set

forth, its technical quality. Unless the artist acquires a skill in manipulating the forms of his craft, his most sensitive insights are likely to be lost upon others. Perhaps the major flaw of thousands of "mute inglorious Milton (s)" is their lack of technical mastery, their ignorance of the rules of their art. The number of really important creative acts, in art or science, which have been performed by fundamentally untutored persons is very small. Just as the physicist must be immersed in the problems of his science for long years before the creative insight occurs, so the artist must be grounded in the problems of his craft, especially in its formal aspects. This is necessary to the exciting creative effort itself, because at the time of discovery the more mundane dimensions of procedure must be already second nature to the creator, else his insight will be clouded over by technical difficulties, perhaps even smothered. The imperative to acquire technique is obviously bound up with the experience of symbol systems. Probably the main way in which formal mastery grows is through a combination of discriminating exposure to past models— the artistic heritage—and a constant exercise of skills based in part upon those models. As the old saw goes, the way to learn how to write is to write. Many technical devices can unquestionably be taught and learned in a deliberate manner. These rules of the game guarantee a certain formal felicity. The question of form itself is not so simple, however; the highest skill is in fact not divorceable from content. It is a part of the art product,

59

an organic component which is involved in the very essence of the created thing. Thus, a particular type of versification can be rationally acquired, while the "ear" of Ezra Pound, his uncanny juxtaposition of sounds, is more than a transferable skill.

The Envisioning of Combinations and Distillations

If one point in the creative process can be singled out as of prepotent significance, it is the moment of vision, when an original formulation occurs to the artist. Without this realization of possibilities for expression, the experiential fund and the technical mastery have no theme upon which to play. The realization may be called insight, inspiration, intuitive flash: it is the feeling of immediate knowledge of connections, of the sight of truth or coherence or pure symmetry. The content of experience becomes meaningful in a selected manner, with such impact that it cries for expression. This occasion cannot be planned or rationally ordered; it seems to happen to the person without his conscious effort, at once a surprise and a fulfillment. The happening is related again and again, by scientists as well as artists, and always with a tone of mystery.[5] It is in the best sense

---

[5] Many examples are quoted by Hutchinson. See, for instance, E. D. Hutchinson, "The Nature of Insight," and other papers by the same author in *A Study of Interpersonal Relations*.

a discovery; because the discovering has been going on for some time in the unconscious, it sometimes appears as a rediscovery of a vision once known and then forgotten. This is the probable basis for Wordsworth's feeling that new insight is a recollection of the divine wisdom of the child.

Perhaps most frequently, the moment of insight embraces a combination of elements of experience. If the segments have previously appeared, they have been unrelated and disparate, but now they suddenly attain an intimate emotional-logical relatedness. Metaphor is a typical example, if the metaphor be of wide and deep implication.

Yet the intuition need not be in the form of connections; it may be a distillation, the intense grasp of essential properties of an object or action. In this guise, it approximates a Platonic recognition of first qualities at the core. For this moment an image or event stands naked before the creative perceiver, revealed in its intensity of being and is-ness.

The great envisioning may take various forms: it may strike as a purely mental flash in a moment of relaxation or dissociation; it may be the end-point of a deep consideration; it may be physically cued by sensory stimuli. The vision of "Kubla Khan" might be an example of the first variety, a long philosophical poem an example of the second, and the chain of associations spurred by Proust's cake and tea an example of the third.

The envisioning may be taken as the starting point

61

of the poem proper. How do authors themselves think verses begin?

Each poem is a unique transaction. Not all poems, even if in the same genre by the same author, begin in an identical manner. In a way each special mood or subject matter imposes its own requirements, the kind of process most congruent with it. At any rate, the starting point is the least fully known of all creative stages. There is substantial agreement that a stimulus of some sort is involved, and apparently this stimulus can be structured in three different modes: (1) it can arise from outside in the form of a striking occurrence or physical object; (2) it can be a combination of outside image and an inner recall, a linking of concrete event with stored memory; or (3) it can be an almost wholly conscious self-stimulation, in which one sets up the goal, intellectually, of writing a poem.

Virtually all poets describe a combination of (1) and (2), abjuring the third process as less significant and less successful. A start *can* be made in the third way by an experienced craftsman, but to the practiced eye it will be an exercise, an imitation poem which lacks integrity. The chief grounding for (1) and (2) is expressed as a *generalized state of awareness,* a heightened consciousness which acts as a prepared ground for stimuli from without and within. As poets comment:[6]

---

[6] Statements in italics are the interview comments of contemporary poets.

62

Keep oneself in readiness for a poem to occur.
Let us be as conscious as possible.
The starting place is a "prepared-for experience."
What happens to stir this awareness, to bring about
the actual crystallization of experience in poetic form?
Poets testify that the stimulus can be almost anything—
a smell, sight, or sound, an unanticipated idea, word, or
image. But they emphasize too the thesis that this specific jog is not entirely isolated from other experience. It
may represent an agglutination of stimuli, a chance
symbolizing of recurrent ideas and emotions. Especially
important is the point that this special occurrence ties
in with past experience, so that memory enters the picture as a crucial variable. The stimulus, to be poetically
transformed, must be connected back to a fund of impressions and valuations. The well, or store of impressions, provides a context in which the immediate experience can be anchored.

Cues come from the memory; a smell or sight, à la
Proust, may release stored impressions.
Childhood impressions are often recalled from when
one's photographic plate was more clear and sensitive.
Childhood experience is strong; it is my freshest file.
The word *inspiration* has a way of complicating this
initial phase of the process. Some poets vow that inspiration is everything; others maintain that what is called
inspiration is really an explicable chain of factors com-
prising the prepared ground, stimulus, and linkage with
the impressionistic fund. Regardless of their degree of

63

adherence to such a concept as inspiration, with its bedrock of mysticism, poets describe the experience itself in similar terms. It consists of a more or less sudden shock by which one immediately and intuitively is thrust into a poetic theme, or better, into a reverie from which such a theme may emerge. There is constant reiteration of the feeling that something "comes," "pings," "bursts," "twists":

A tune came.

I seldom search for anything, but let it come to me.

Short poems spring quickly into consciousness, often after awakening in the morning.

There is a burst, a visitation. In one stark experience the poem comes as a whole.

A poem is a spasm, a shock, twisting open the unconscious.

There is an initial strong feeling about a subject; this immediate conception starts one off.

Inspiration is invaluable . . . some initial attraction, which may never recur.

Two cases may be cited as striking examples of the inspired beginning, demonstrating the total impact of poetic genesis. Richard Eberhart states that he has a poor memory and must jot down his thoughts as they arise. He looks upon the beginning of a poem as a gift. At times the words pour out. "The Groundhog," perhaps his best-known poem, was written in half an hour. One group of his poems was written in the middle of the night. He got out of bed, jotted down lines on three-by-five slips; the result was twenty six-line poems in one hour, their form dictated by the size of the paper at hand. The late Gene Derwood stressed the fact that the poem was a total experience, involving her entire mind and body. She felt that the poem started as a shock, speeding up all her activities, "like a kick in the solar plexus." She often experienced intense physical excitement for several days, sometimes suffering a severe heart spasm at the poem's completion.

This phase of the process is of course not necessarily a guarantee that a finished poem will result. Although the immense jump has been made, and some poems such as Eberhart's "Groundhog" may be almost instantaneously complete, the art work itself has typically scarcely begun. The vision must be shaped and clothed, formed into an artistic whole. The vast thrill of the conception waits upon a mature execution. The unconscious has done its most important duty. Although the great energies of unconscious forces will be called on again and again throughout the process, they have here performed their most notable function, and the one least susceptible to rational control.

Elucidation of the Vision

The vision must be shaped and made tangible if it is to be successfully communicated. There is a conscious application of energy to the task of making the combination or distillation meaningful. The task involves an explication of the insightful moment in such a way that its character becomes significant, both to the creator himself and to his potential audience. Here the technical facility acts as a reagent upon the visionary mass, giving it a discernible structure. In Schneider's terms, creative "thrust" from the unconscious is broken to the bit of creative "mastery," in which the conscious self, oriented to reality, is of first importance. The artist must endure the inevitable disharmony between conception and execution, and attempt to recapture as much of his insight as he possibly can. The personal relevance of the period of intuition must be transformed into a broader relevance in this era of elucidation, the words made socially significant while retaining their distinctive idiosyncratic overtones.[7] This is the key point of Rank's "will to form": the will exerts itself toward the attainment of a suitable structure for the imaginative insight,

---

[7] Otto Rank derives the essential creative act from a consideration of language in its social and individual characteristics. Discussing the historical parallels of Christianity and art, Rank says that "a power of new creation by speech is vouchsafed to every individual. It is only later that the poet comes to perform it for the rest and he does so by harmonious fusion of the individual and collective forces, for though it is a language of his own, and therewith a world of his own, that he builds, it is yet such that it conveys something to others and helps them to build a world of their own."

and insists upon imposing the order of artistic criteria on the loosely given vision.[8]

But elucidation of a predetermined insight is not the sole occurrence at this stage. The maker of an art product does not suddenly stop and merely impose form on a given set of images or ideas. The creative process is fluid; it persists in giving rise to novelty at each stage of the creator's development. And so, when the artistic creation is in the shaping stage, it may be quickly illumined by a further insight of the nature described above. Discoveries take place at every point; the poem shapes itself by suggesting its own further progress. The word used to convey a specific idea keys off a chain of other ideas which may be immediately applicable to the course of the work at hand. The never-ending processes of association may turn up surprising things for the poet.[9]

---

[8] In Richard Wilbur's words: "In general, I would say that limitation makes for power: the strength of the genie comes from his being confined in a bottle." (*Mid-Century American Poets.*)

[9] Robert Frost, in his essay "The Figure a Poem Makes," expresses this "discovery" element: "It must be a revelation, or a series of revelations, as much for the poet as for the reader. . . . A poem may be worked over once it is in being, but may not be worried into being. Its most precious quality will remain its having run itself and carried away the poet with it."

At this stage of elucidation, the artist comes to terms with reality in the psychological sense. This is not to say that he compromises the vision, but that in making it socially meaningful he demonstrates an element of control, a discrimination between pure fantasy and the demands of the concrete world "out there." He returns to a psychological state of grace which distinguishes him from the psychotic who lives in an illusion and the neurotic who is incapable of self-mastery. He proves that his psychic azimuth is directed not to a world of dissociated illusion but to the real world, even though it is a unique perception of the world, enhanced and informed by the power of the dream.[10]

Elucidation embraces the conscious effort to shape lines of verse on paper in such a way that they transmit the poet's full intent. Poets report that this process of working through their material is a combination of conscious and unconscious strivings, but that rational mastery is relatively more important here than in the previous stage of envisioning or inspiration.

The first draft of a poem may consume a few hours or several days. It must be recognized that, in all but a few cases, the poem does not arise full-blown in direct

---

[10] The artist's conscious mastery is emphasized especially by Lionel Trilling in his important and extraordinarily perceptive paper, "Art and Neurosis," in *The Liberal Imagination.*

consequence of the stimulating experience. Rather, it is keyed to the experience, and to the vital word or phrase which first symbolized that experience, but goes on to develop in its own way.[11] One might say that most poems are like complicated chemical reactions, in which the outcome is uncertain but each occurrence sets off another, related occurrence. The working-through falls conveniently into two phases, the first draft formulation (which may in some cases be the finished poem) and the subsequent revision and polishing. It has been pointed out that the first draft is in part a voyage of discovery, in which the poem grows by associations to, and refinements of, the original key symbol and each successive extension. There is a suggestion that the poem has a certain autonomy, that it fulfills itself according to subtle patterns of growth:

> *The process of writing a poem is like climbing a mountain . . . steep, although there are easy spots. The unanticipated insight is most important; one comes upon it in the ascent up the mountain. Every image should evoke another image.*

---

[11] "Paul Valéry speaks of the 'une ligne donnée' of a poem. One line is given to the poet by God or by nature, the rest he has to discover for himself." (Stephen Spender, "The Making of a Poem," in *Critiques and Essays in Criticism*).

During a long "murmuring period" the lines work themselves out and I repeat them audibly, voicing my progress.

The poem develops as a musical structure. There is an eagerness to fulfill the phrase. Each thing suggests another; one doesn't know in advance what he's going to do. The poem is an environment. The poem may be compared to the dance. There is the same repetition of learned steps, and a consistency of overtones.

There is a feeling of confidence that the poem will shape itself to an end. After its genesis in a particular emotional experience, the poem moves away from the concrete, is "transvalued" so that it gains a general dimension.

Many poets consider revision to be perhaps the most salient portion of the creative process. The emphasis is on technique, craft, and patient work. One is here one's own critic, and may be exceedingly harsh, demanding a score (or more) of rewritings. In Marianne Moore's aphorism, "rewriting is rewarding." This phase of the effort is highly sophisticated, drawing heavily on the poet's artistic experience and his linguistic virtuosity. Yet there is a hint in the poets' comments that revision is more than a conscious working over of material; the strain of exactitude may in fact stir the unconscious springs of expression to new oscillations and taut precisions:

70

Writing a poem is mostly revision; new insights may come during the revision, the poem may change entirely. In revision, one gets closer to, not further from, the unconscious.

If value cannot be transferred, of what value is it? Craftsmanship is indispensable and actually inseparable from value to be conveyed.

Revision is the most important part of writing. The real work lies in judging and reforming initial lines. There is a sense of competition, of striving toward an impersonal standard, like par in golf.

Revision entails, often, an entirely fresh rewriting since each word must fit the whole structure of the poem.

The End of the Poem and Its Meaning to the Poet

The final stage to be abstracted from the creative process is barely distinguishable from the fourth. It is the reappraisal of what has gone before, the last intimate probing which completes the art product. Here the patina is added to a rough-hewn creation through censorship, revision, and close attention to details of technical perfection. This stage is not always vital; the poem, in certain cases, may arise full-blown from the initial visionary elucidation, as in the instance, again, of "Kubla Khan." But often such a last step may find the brick that fulfills the artist's mosaic, a particular word or phrase long-sought but for a considerable time unattain-

71

able. Thus A. E. Housman describes a poem of which several stanzas came to him in the first elucidation, while the last stanza was more akin to literary carpentry and required several efforts.

Here the spectator self, the other observer internalized, functions to enhance the communicability of the art product. Self-criticism opens up the poem for an aesthetic reappraisal, and leads to changes which may increase clarity, adding point and force to the creation. One might conceive of an artistic conscience energized by the pride of craft, so that no aspect emerges in the final version which is less perfect than possible. Of course artists may vary greatly in their self-demandingness, from the person who spews forth a great volume of work relatively unchecked by critical conscience to the true perfectionist whose constant rewording brings him only to what he regards as a heightened approximation to desirable form.

What does the writer feel he gains from his poem, and how does he regard the finished effort? The question of reward is an intriguing one, since it is clear that modern poets, with very few exceptions, can anticipate neither riches nor fame. The answer can only be, "Because I like to do it," or, "Because I have to do it." The pleasure of writing itself, the intrinsically rewarding quality of poetry, is at the heart of creative endeavor.

The poet's reward is derived from the poem itself.

The personal, not grandiose, pleasure of hooking an

idea, of getting it trapped in words, is perhaps more elating than actually finishing the poem.

Why do dancers dance?

Self-assertion is often given as a reason for writing, the hope that one will master his medium and gain appropriate recognition, and the more distant hope that one will achieve a measure of immortality:

Ego-assertion is a part of writing poetry; one wants to capture one perfect thing, to survive after the bubble breaks.

Finally, some poets state that poetry is for them a release from psychic tensions:

Poetry is a release for the psyche.

It fills the need to "get it out." It afforded a release of grief after my wife's death; even sad poetry gives its own pleasurable feeling.

What are the feelings which accompany the completion of a creative task? The most frequently mentioned state is one of pleasure, elation, even exultation:

There is a feeling of catharsis and exhilaration.

There is elation at the completion of form.

It is a satisfaction to have stated it, to have gotten it—a joy that "they can't take that away from me."

There is a good feeling after the poem is out, a desire to read it aloud, to show it to people.

The normal feeling should be one of exhilaration, tempered with anxiety.

The other major theme concerns the necessity of leaving the work behind, in order to get on with new efforts:

There is a first flush on completion; one should then forget about it forever.

A poem is never finished. It is abandoned in despair.

Poets are, then, largely in agreement about the way a poem is made. It is psychologically appropriate to believe that the creative personality is related in a meaningful way to this process.

The Poet's Personality

The personalities of individuals who write good poetry are probably as diverse as those of physicians or businessmen. There is no simple one-to-one relationship between the requirements of a craft and the psychological pattern of the craftsman. But this is not to say that certain characteristics are not more commonly associated with one social role than with another. The distribution of talents and tasks in society is never a purely random affair; human beings are not interchangeable parts in some grand social machine. People prefer one job rather than another, and the demands of the job fit more or less closely with different sorts of personality. This "fit" is the core of the effort to demonstrate how the poet's personal dispositions are related to his total performance of the artistic role.

74

There is reason to believe that the artist is more intimately involved in his vocation than are members of most other occupations. Poetry is a total job, in the sense that his work is in a very real way the poet's life. Virtually any profession other than art or pure science meets one of two descriptions: it is centered on certain defined human relationships, as in medicine, or it deals with a restricted subject matter whose boundaries may be clearly stated, as in engineering. The poet, however, works with the material of life in all its complexity and richness, and most importantly with his own life: his experiences, perceptions, values. He constantly draws upon himself and meets the outer world with only the tools of his own essential humanity. Of course he possesses some technical aids, his knowledge of verse forms and strategies of expression. Yet even the language he employs, although socially given, is his own, a part of his humanity because it has been given his personal stamp and flavor. The poet must thus be viewed against his art before he can be viewed against his society.

Plato and Aristotle may be taken as twin origins of the traditional ideas about the creative personality. One long stream of development, as Otto Rank notes, has tended to emphasize the creative talent as an unconscious, instinctive gift:

For Plato—with whom the philosophy of aesthetic, as of so much else really begins, the poet—we should add, the Greek poet—is wholly an instrument of the divine; his faculty is purely

75

> instinctive and unconscious. . . . Plato not only
> neglects the role of consciousness, but com-
> pletely eliminates it, putting in its place mania,
> a being outside oneself, a divine inspiration.

Aristotle, on the other hand, emphasizes the rational aspects of poetry and locates its source in the poet's instincts for imitation and harmony. The *Poetics* reveal his concern with aesthetic symmetry and his concentration on the logical canons of tragic drama. Yet he too, despite his recognition of conscious craftsmanship, finally traces poetic activity to something given and instinctive: "Hence," he says, "poetry implies either a special gift of nature or a strain of madness."

It seems certain that the creative process is a blend of unconscious "push" or inspiration and deliberate control of the material for an artistic purpose. No clean split can be made between these aspects; they fuse in the actual working-out of the poem, although they may differ in intensity at different stages of the process. Traditional conceptions of the poet's personality may be seen, in greatly over-simplified terms, as a debate between those who stress one of these two major elements at the expense of the other. These shifting emphases, for instance, seem very important in the development of classical and romantic literary philosophies. The categories of classical and romantic no longer seem very pertinent in literary criticism, since they have been worn by excessive and contradictory use. But it may be possible to discern in them central meanings which have a bearing on the various ideas about the creative personality.

The classical view emphasizes conscious elaboration of an art form, refined by technical planning and polishing according to rather well-defined formal criteria of appropriateness and excellence. The romantic position tends instead to stress the flow of images from the unconscious and the role of the artist as the creature of his inspirations. Here the poet is vehicle or vessel for a relatively "spontaneous" generation of the poem. Classical theory deals almost exclusively with the properties of the poem, while romantic conceptions often focus on the relation between the poem and its creator, devoting much attention to the poet as person.

In the classical tradition, from Aristotle to the poetry, drama, and criticism of eighteenth-century France and England, the rules of art are primary, and the artistic personality is not of any particular interest except as it dovetails with formal properties of poetry as a craft. The poet is primarily a conscious master of symbols whose insight must be shaped to conform to a strict scheme of presentation. At its most extreme, we think of the unities of French drama, the poetic practice of a Racine or a Samuel Johnson.

The romantic thread courses from Plato through Rousseau to the English writers of the early nineteenth century who are specifically called romantic. Shelley, Keats, Wordsworth, and Coleridge may be taken as exemplars. The artist is often seen as one who uses himself, who relies more heavily on an internal burst of inspiration than on critical dicta about the proper treatment of themes. Raw material for a poem springs up from within and is then clothed in an acceptable vestment of style. If reason is the classical ideal, in art as in life, emotion is the romantic keynote. Whether the emotion is recollected in tranquillity or poured out in frenzy, some personal emotional response is paramount. The attention to subjective and non-rational aspects of creativity reaches its zenith in the deliberate titillation of the senses by drugs, the abdication of conscious mastery, practiced by certain romantic poets.

In one sense, of course, the "problem" of the poet's personality is singular to our own place and time. Curiosity about the psychological patterns of the artist has been especially intense in the Western world since the Renaissance; the anonymous art of feudal Europe and the semi-anonymous poetry of classical China illustrate that such curiosity is not inevitable in an art or in a society. Yet many observers have tried to characterize the poet during the past century and a half, and it may be helpful to review some of their suggestions before listening to the comments of contemporary poets.

Coleridge, despite his position among the romantic poets with their exaltation of the unconscious phase of the creative dialectic, set down in *Biographia Literaria* an exceedingly well-rounded picture of poetic activity:

The poet, described in ideal perfection, brings the whole soul of man into activity, with the

78

subordination of its faculties to each other, according to their relative worth and dignity. He diffuses a tone and spirit of unity, that blends, and (as it were) fuses, each into each, by that synthetic and magical power, to which we have exclusively appropriated the name of imagination. This power, first put in action by the will and understanding, and retained under their irremissive, though gentle and unnoticed, control (laxis effertur habenis) reveals itself in the balance or reconciliation of opposite or discordant qualities: of sameness, with difference; the individual, with the representative; the sense of novelty and freshness, with old and familiar objects, a more than usual state of emotion, with more than usual order; judgment ever awake and steady self-possession, with enthusiasm and feeling profound or vehement. . .

Coleridge did not bow before the poet as an eternal mystery; he felt that creativity could be described and explained, and proceeded to apply his principles in the analysis of Shakespeare. As I. A. Richards points out, he believed that writing a poem "is *activity;* poetry is something the poet does, not something done to him." Noting the combination of disparate things by the imaginative power which unified and reconciled, Coleridge attributed this power to the will and understanding, thus crediting the poet with a high degree of conscious control. By relating emotion and order, enthusiasm and judgment,

79

he affirmed that these various qualities were all necessary to the total creative act.

Few have portrayed the poet with such grandeur as
Carlyle did in examining "The Hero as Poet." Underlying his mystical conception of the writer's role are two
themes which are critical in the search for basic elements
of creative personality: vision and intelligence. Carlyle's
treatment of vision singled out the idea of the poet as
prophet; infatuated with the mystic cadences of German
philosophy, he assigned the poet the task of revealing
the "divine mystery of the universe," of enunciating
Goethe's "open secret." The description of the poet as
seer becomes quite complicated, because while he is
demonstrably ultra-perceptive, an acute observer, this
fact gets entangled with the other connotation of seer
as a person capable of intuitively kenning the future. At
any rate, Carlyle stresses the accuracy of perception:
"poetic creation, what is this too but *seeing* the thing
sufficiently." It is interesting that Carlyle, while clinging
to his theory of a cosmic sensitivity in the poet, did not
neglect the cognitive aspects of the art. While others
perhaps take intelligence for granted in discussing the
poet's make-up, he explicitly states: "At bottom, it is
the Poet's first gift, as it is all men's, that he have intellect
enough."

Perhaps the most extreme romantic position on poetic
activity and personality is found in Emerson's lyrical
account. He reiterates several of Coleridge's and Carlyle's
insights, remarking especially the poet's wholeness, sen-

sitivity, and perceptual capacity. He sees the poet as one who is extraordinarily receptive to the stimuli which most men overlook or register only faintly: "Too feeble fall the impressions of nature on us to make us artists. Every touch should thrill." This sensitivity is the condition of the poet's clear vision. Emerson conceives of the artist as expressing a beauty and symmetry which are objectively given in nature, but which most of us are unable to recognize. The poet is then able to articulate what he sees, to capture it in words: "the poet is the Namer or Language-maker." One notes again the great stress on language as more than a tool, as a part of the poet's work and personality style. Emerson allies himself with those who think of the poet as a person who gives himself up to inspiration. He speaks of "a new energy" which comes to a man "by abandonment to the nature of things." The poet "knows that he speaks adequately then only when he speaks somewhat wildly—; not with the intellect used as an organ, but with the intellect released from all service and suffered to take its direction from its celestial life."

Thus Emerson brings us back to the original dialectic of rational and non-rational by his emphasis on the poet's subjection to the vast forces of life: id, unconscious, celestial life. With the development, since Freud, of a set of theories concerned with the potent role of unconscious mental content in human behavior, increased attention to the problems of artistic creativity was inevitable. For psychoanalytic thought set as part of its task

81

the elucidation of psychic activity which had been neglected in most of the older views of man, the views of philosophers, historians, economists, and critics. Yet this very activity—the working of forces not open to the individual's conscious control and examination—had been intimately involved in the consideration of creative effort. Since Plato, men had sensed their importance, and of these men it was the artists themselves, as Freud noted, who "discovered" the unconscious and knew of its significance in their lives and work.

Psychoanalytic views of the poet's personality have decidedly focused on unconscious forces, but there has been little agreement about either the nature of those forces or the way in which they eventuate in artistic work. Freud and Jung were both pessimistic about the possibility of explaining artistic creativity in psychological terms, since they were very sensitive to the distinction between the dreams and fantasies of the non-creative person and the socially valued, styled imagination of the artist.

Freud's dictum that "psychoanalysis must lay down its arms before the problem of the poet" was based on his conviction that artistic talent and productivity were linked to sublimation, or the re-direction of instinctual forces into socially acceptable channels. Sublimation is a process which he never succeeded in analyzing to his own or others' satisfaction; he saw it as biologically rooted and hence inaccessible to psychological inquiry. Despite Freud's unwillingness to advance an easy formula for the poet's work, however, his writings abound in casual insights. The most significant of these is probably his comparison between art and daydreams, in which he recognizes the fundamental point that the poet, unlike the mentally ill person—or, for that matter, the normal day-dreamer—makes his return to the real world by clothing his dreams in socially perceptible and treasured form. Freud's general importance to the understanding of the artist was undoubtedly contained in his basic contribution to human thought: the explication of the unconscious in all its pervasive influence on behavior. As Trilling has seen, "Freud, by the whole tendency of his psychology, establishes the *naturalness* of artistic thought." What earlier observers had considered a closed mystery—the poet's talent for using the substance of his unconscious—may now be accepted as a point, a very high point indeed, on the normal range of human function. We all possess unconscious energies, and while the poet is more vigorously aware of his own power and is technically trained, we are no longer forced to think of him as being apart. Freud then brings the poet closer by revealing that creator and non-creator share some common experience of themselves, and by demonstrating that the artist in his most excellent moment is related in his humanity to all men.

The content of art does not, in Jung's opinion, spring mainly from the personality of the individual artist. Rather, he sees the created work as an expression of the culture in which the artist moves; at its most profound it is a magnificent representation of "archetypes," or collective human themes which reside in the mind and memory of the race. Poetic symbolism is not derived from unique events in the poet's life but from certain universal meanings attached to man's experience. The problem of the poet's psychology is thus not in itself a practical or desirable object of study, since the poet serves as a social voice and is truly impersonal while pursuing the artistic task. ("In his capacity of artist he is neither auto-erotic, nor hetero-erotic, nor erotic in any sense. He is objective and impersonal—even inhuman—for as an artist he is his work and not a human being.") So far is Jung, like Freud, from proposing any simple equation between personality pattern and artistic result that he too "lays down his arms." His reasoning, however, introduces a new theme by indicating that our usual scientific approach to behavior handicaps the study of the poet by its exclusive concern with responses to situations rather than original activity:

> Any reaction to stimulus may be causally explained; but the creative act, which is the absolute antithesis of mere reaction, will forever elude the human understanding.

Other psychoanalytic thinkers, notably Otto Rank, have been somewhat more optimistic about the possibility of comprehending the poet's craft. Rank's *Art and Artist* is perhaps the most exhaustive psychological treatment of the problems of creativity; its sweeping analysis demonstrates that art, from primitive body decoration to elaborate drama or painting, is an integral part of human life. Rank affirms two basic assumptions underlying the present discussion, namely that creativity embraces conscious and unconscious elements, and that language plays a central role in the poetic enterprise. He further succeeds in tying these assumptions together in his analysis of the creative act. He holds that individual creativity begins with the idea of a poem, and that this idea, powered by the unconscious, comprises unrefined words and images. But this is only the first step; when the poem is transformed into an intelligible product, when communication is foremost, then the conscious aspects of personality hold sway:

So the poetic process divides more or less clearly into two separate phases, which have been called the conscious and the unconscious, but which really correspond to the two processes of language-formation, the individual creative expression of an experience and the collective communication of it.

Rank also attacks the question of the artist's mental health or illness by proposing that art is in some sense a substitute for creative living. Since "there can be no doubt that the great works of art were bought at the cost of ordinary living," the highest fulfillment of the personality in action would require a withdrawal from artistic creativity. The exclusive concern with individual psychic health as it works itself out in concrete interpersonal relations, a concern typical of contemporary society, has led many more recent psychoanalytic theorists to attempt "explanations" of the artist in terms of specific neurotic mechanisms.

Among contemporary theorists of the artistic personality only Daniel Schneider, himself a novelist, seems to retain the broad view and generous spirit toward art which was so characteristic of early psychoanalysts. In *The Psychoanalyst and the Artist* he concentrates on the creative process and enriches our conception of the poet's task. He reiterates the interplay of unconscious and conscious forces, but wisely avoids labeling the poet with any single psychological conflict or emotional disability. Schneider describes, in a manner reminiscent of Rank, the confluence of individual and social patterns in artistic work:

> Consequently, artistic technique, at its highest and most enduring, is the work of interpretive transformation of the individual unconscious into a universalized expression, accessible to the mass of people, of all the forces, personal and social, which impinge upon human consciousness.

He goes on to emphasize the dialectic of intuitive upsurge and conscious rational mastery of the artist's material:

> We tentatively defined artistic (and creative scientific) thinking as a combination of intuition and cognition and showed why, in the powerful creative intelligence, these two factors must meet

86

and interlock with each other; otherwise the unconscious could never influence the *form* of conscious thinking nor could cognition itself ever penetrate the unconscious.

Other current views of the artist often seem markedly parochial because they are derived from psychotherapeutic work with neurotic patients who happened also to be artists or would-be artists. Two typical formulations are those of Lee and Bergler, both practising analysts who number several painters and writers among their clients. Lee believes that the artist suffers from a "destructive rage" and that his poem or picture is an unconsciously dictated means of overcoming this rage and regaining mental balance. He states that "the created work is something made to bridge the way back to mental health from the despondency into which the artist's destructive rage has plunged him." It is thus not an end in itself, but a mechanism of restitution: "The artist creates in answer to an unconscious need to relieve his suffering by extricating himself from a mobile depression brought on by the expression of unreasonable destructive rage." But what are the origins of this consuming rage with which the artist, a neurotically ill person, must cope? Lee traces it to two prepotent needs, those for excessive self-regard and for a special relation to women, which are inevitably thwarted. While he is willing to admit that there are many varieties of artist and types of aesthetic experience, all are underlain by a common theme of creativity as a defense against rage.

87

Bergler's thesis is even more assured and specific than Lee's. He proposes unequivocally that the writer is ill, and that his illness follows one exclusive pattern limited to artistically creative people. The writer, he states, feels deprived of his mother's nurturance and fears that she will reject him. As a defense against this fear, the writer takes on the roles of both mother and son within himself; he "feeds" himself and proves his self-sufficiency by creating a work of art. Bergler concludes that, "The poet can express nothing but inner defenses against his inner conflicts," and that there is no such thing as a normal writer.

The absurdity of such myths as that the poet is "nothing but" a particular kind of neurotic is readily apparent. They rest on the fallacies of drawing mountainous generalizations from selected case-history molehills and of regarding the poet without the poetry. Yet these arrogant shrinkings of genius into a neurotic mold do serve the purpose of alerting us to a question of genuine interest. The possible relations between artistry and illness have long fascinated the artist and critic as well as the psychologist. The idea that internal conflict, a restlessness and thirst for new experience, urges the poet on is well-known and plausible. Perhaps even more intriguing, however, and more in keeping with our stress on the interplay between the creative process and the personalities engaged in it, is the idea that poetry-making itself imposes certain necessary strains on the poet.

Although Plato spoke of the poet's divine madness, it

was not until the romantic era that people seriously began to think of him as a congenital misfit. As Trilling remarks, he "was always known to belong to a touchy tribe," but few had considered him mentally ill. The tendency to regard the poet as ill may be linked to the rise of his traditional "alienation" from society. Turnell charts the alienation as coincident with growing middle-class political dominance and the breakdown of the patronage system, changes which were at their peak around the beginning of the nineteenth century. If the poet became "declassed" and unwanted, his irregular position in society was perhaps relevant to the theory that he was psychologically disturbed; individuals who are somewhat at odds with the existing social order may find themselves summarily classified as ill.

The psychological derogation of the artist became acute in such writers as Lombroso and Max Nordau. The latter's account of "the degeneracy of art" was answered by Bernard Shaw in his essay, "The Sanity of Art"; this polemical theme, so different in spirit from the awe in which previous ages had held the poet, seems to carry down to the present day. And Trilling testifies that it is indeed a singular development:

> The eighteenth century did not find the poet to be less than other men, and certainly the Renaissance did not . . . . the Renaissance ideal held poetry to be, like arms or music, one of the signs of manly competence.

89

Kretschmer sums up the evidence for "madness" theories in this fashion:

> Only this much can one say: that mental disease, and more especially, those ill-defined conditions on the boundary of mental disease, are decidedly more frequent among men of genius, at least in certain groups, than they are among the general population.

He elaborates the argument by noting that the highest-achieving artist, the true genius, is characterized by a fusion of instability and sanity, so that there is "a significant give-and-take of the psychopathic component with the firmly integrated mass of the healthy, total personality."

Hutchinson, after extensive study of scientific creativity, advances the idea that the creative process itself involves a phase in which mental imbalance is likely to be paramount:

> Inherent in the very process of creation— inherent, that is, in the necessary delays, frustrations, and ineptitudes of the Period of Renunciation—are the seeds of defeat and self-destruction. Suffering, the substance of all that is mentally injurious, is an almost inevitable prelude to success.[2]

The fact that many men of genius suffer from psychic disorder obviously does not prove that insanity is the condition of creative work or that every creative person must be mentally disordered. It may illustrate that "one phase of the creative process has inherent in it a potential pathology." If the process imposes strain, then the possible occurrence of mental illness rests on the individual artist's capacity for tolerating that strain and turning it toward the goal of a finished poem.

It has been remarked that one source of the rigors the artist undergoes in his work may be found in the culture to which he is heir. Conflicts are "given" by the assumptions and traditions of Western society; everyone is exposed to them, but they impinge on the artist with peculiar force because of his heightened sensitivity. These conflicts often take the form of the basic dualisms cited by L. L. Whyte, such as mind-matter or objective-subjective, or the gulf, adduced by Heller in his analysis of privacy in modern poetry, between symbol and reality. Whyte insists that these irreconcilable conceptions are presented to every man, but that they may lead to neurosis in all but the strongest artists since the artists experience them more intensely.

Finally, before turning to the specific implications of poetic creativity for personality, and the comments of contemporary poets on the artist's psychology, it is important to observe that some artists have themselves contributed to the stereotype of the poet as deranged. Certain Romantics and late nineteenth-century French poets, especially, deliberately fostered the fiction of the artist's degeneracy by their emphasis on unusual varieties of sensory titillation and extreme styles of life. Some critics have accepted the idea of the artist's disability and turned it into a peculiar virtue. These are writers who champion the arts and view neurosis as the poet's glory. Edmund Wilson advances such a theory, using the story of Philoctetes as a powerful metaphorical clue. The artist, like Philoctetes, nurses a wound which ordinary society finds disagreeable. Yet he has a magic "bow" —his art—which makes him immeasurably valuable to society at certain times. He is therefore condemned to retain his disability, and so to get along badly in his interpersonal relations, as a sort of "price" for the exercise of the creative gift.

To the aesthetically alert person, this explanation has a vivid appeal; it evokes our admiration for the individual who strives and succeeds despite his handicap, and sets the poet out as a glorious misfit. Yet it may be unnecessary to view the poet as inherently ill, to make neurosis a precondition of artistic worth. Even if one grants that artists show a disproportionate amount of the kind of behavior our society calls illness—and this is an unproved assumption, because it is likely that the ill artist is merely better known than ill persons in other occupations—it is not inevitable that the poet's personality itself be seen as the center of disturbance. We may instead return to the creative process, as Hutchinson and others suggest, and link the hardy nature of the poetic enterprise to the psychological difficulties the poet may face.

92

The imperatives of the creative process center around two kinds of strength in the personality. The process is complicated and, fully considered in life terms, very long. So the person must have sufficient vitality to carry out a lengthy job of accretion and formation. Although a play-function certainly exists, artists bear testimony to the fact that art is work. The artist needs more than the energy required for routine living, enough more so that he can project a part of himself out into the created object. In addition to this sheer vitality and exuberance, a kind of integrative strength is required. One might term this balance, capacity for adjustment, or ego-strength. At any rate, the artist is one who uses himself mercilessly, who rakes and strains at his inner dynamic, deliberately provoking elements of conflict and terror within. He may not prod the unconscious, as certain of the romantic poets did, with alcohol or laudanum, but he prods it. (Incidentally, references to "it," "the thing," and "my neurosis" are legion among poets and fit well with the literal translation of the title of Freud's book, *Das Ich und das Es,* The I and the It.) Karl Shapiro writes in *Poets at Work* that "the poet is different from the non-poet in that he makes greater demands on his Unknown than anyone else, and that he brings to light certain riches which are accorded a universal value."

The element of integrative strength leads into the next important component, which is a capacity for perceiving associations among things or ideas, linking them at times and at other times holding them balanced

93

in conflict. A largeness, a generosity toward impressions, enables the creator to accept irreconcilable modes, resolving them if he can, but encompassing them if necessary under the rubric of self. That is, the artist may recognize multiple meanings and enjoy them in their variety. As he associates the dissimilar, he may dissociate the similar, peeling off layers of meaning or "types of ambiguity," as William Empson has termed them. He can perceive in more than one way, especially in other ways than the conventional ones. This too requires a kind of strength and breadth of perspective, for the tension between widely various ideas must be maintained without compromise, without arbitrarily narrowing one's vision in the interests of psychic ease.

As the foundation for creative activity, the poet needs a certain type of sensitivity; he is permeable to impressions. This is a schooled sensitivity, one in which keen and discriminating observation are more vital than mere gross impressionability.

If his impressions are to become meaningful to others, then they must be *formed* artistically. A desire to capture the essential character of a person, situation, or mood is typically a poetic desire. Here is the chief significance of the traditional concern with words on the poet's part. As Auden writes in *Poets at Work*, the poet loves language for its own sake, and:

> Whether this love is a sign of his poetic gift
> or the gift itself—for falling in love is given
> not chosen—I don't know, but it is certainly the

94

sign by which one recognizes whether a young man is potentially a poet or not.

Infatuated with words, the poet wills communication, and if the aim of explicating the obvious or subtle is not there, then works of art will not be forthcoming, and the person is not performing the full poetic role. It is well to remember that in the "explication" phase, the poet need not necessarily be writing for a public or even for one other person; most usually, he is not, but in making something clear to the social self within—the spectator self—he will thereby make it meaningful to *some* others. (If his work contained no clues for *any* other observer, then it would be schizophrenic art, whose value is diagnostic, not aesthetic.)

A summing up of the imperatives for the creative personality shows certain characteristics essential to the functioning poet. Whatever his particular personality pattern may be, he cannot be understood fully without reference to the following technical "boundaries": *strength* (both vitality and ego-strength or integrative strength); *a capacity for association and integration* (of ideas and images—a generosity toward impressions and ability to encompass tensions); *sensitivity* (discriminant permeability); *a desire for form and explication* (linguistic facility or infatuation with words); and *intelligence*. Regarding the last of these characteristics, it is obvious that the role requires a rather large portion of what is ordinarily called intelligence. But above a certain level of competence, the concept of raw I.Q. means very little.

95

A poetic intellect is not the same as a scientific intellect, alhough they share a common baseline of better-than-average mental functioning. I have been speaking here of particular parts of intelligence as seen in their significance for the artist; they happen to be the special forms which his intelligence takes.

The responses of poets to the question of what constitutes the personality necessary for artistic creativity tend to support the foregoing assumptions, although in modified form. The poet as person, affirm the artists, is interesting but superfluous. The best of the man is in his work, and the work is the key question in artistic activity. Nevertheless, there is a series of requisites which must be fulfilled in the poetically creative personality as ideal type. Any one poet may show certain features and fail almost completely to manifest certain others, but each must approach a core complex of capacities which underlies the vagaries of individual personality make-ups. The characteristics of poets are indeed various. Experience with practicing artists impels one to cast aside nearly every initial generalization which might be made concerning overt personality traits, such as: poets are very introverted, fairly extroverted; very effeminate, very masculine; simple livers, lovers of luxury; aggressively irritable, benevolently kind. Yet when called upon to designate characteristics which they felt were crucial to poetic endeavor, or at least exceedingly germane, the poets evidenced remarkable agreement.

Both the wide variety of qualities singled out and

their close relations to one another suggest that they might best be considered as a system of capacities. There is no one psychological style fitted to include or explain the characteristics without forcing them into a mold which would violate the facts. At the same time, the variety is not infinite, and it is soon apparent that more than random listing is involved. It seems best, then, to emphasize that the personality make-up judged most desirable tends to approximate a pattern; this pattern has form without being extremely close-knit or exhaustive.

Four outstanding capacities may be staked out for consideration, and on these poets are quite well agreed. These are the capacities for *experience,* for *ordering experience,* for *exploring and using one's own personality,* and for the *use of language.* A fifth area is essential to this report, but on this area there are crucial disagreements; this is the question of whether the work of the poet requires a *harmoniously organized personality* or *an imbalance of personality.*

The Capacity for Experience

The stress here is upon sensitivity, intensity, awareness, and enthusiasm. A poet must have great curiosity about people and natural objects, an attachment to the world so intense that his satiation point for experience is above most other men's. Included too is the capacity for absorbing shock, for flexibility of mind:

> *A poet must have enthusiasm for life, for what you encounter in the world.*

97

There must be sensibility: a more highly nervous organization of personality.

He should possess the capacity for living at a higher pitch: spontaneous combustion, effervescence. Also, he should have empathy, intuition—the ability immediately to understand other people, even if he doesn't like them.

There should be a capacity for a general awareness of humanity, complete association with society: all humanity are his relatives.

The acute awareness is partly physical. I recall how upset Robert Frost was by his having drunk a cup of tea pressed upon him by his hostess after he had first refused it.

He should have the feeling of being more alive, of being able to experience life at several segments and levels.

There must be an ability to live more than others, not to become bored or satiated.

He should have "imagination," a marvelous "forgetter," the ability to scrub his brain clean and come up fresh.

The Capacity for Ordering Experience

The poet desires to shape and objectify experience, but first and most vitally to somehow capture it. Paramount in this drive for order and experiential conquest is a kind of detachment which complements the deep attachment of the experience itself. It is as if one had to move away from, and precisely represent, the idea, image, or feeling which had occurred. There is the notion of strict honesty toward the materials of poetry. In ordering experience one must not distort it:

The poet must shape the materials offered: "objectism."

He should be dissociated from community life, "out of the swim," in order to gain perspective.

There must be a desire for a savage intensity of analysis.

Ideally, he should have docility, reflectiveness, tenacity of mind and act.

The Capacity for Exploring and Using One's Own Personality

Honesty toward the self, and a desire to probe the secrets of the self, are essential. Self-focusing is accompanied by a certain inwardness and egoism. Some egoism and neglect of others is implied by the necessity for self-regard. If many poets are too close to their work to live agreeably with others, it must be remembered that part of their work is self-exploration. An element of tough-mindedness is involved, since a penetrating look at the self must be accepted without flinching.

The poets interviewed commented as follows:

One must have toughness of character.

The poet is intimately concerned with his own personality. Unlike the "objective" scientist, he gnaws at his vitals. The poet is the spider with a web coming out of its belly.

A created work is nothing more than an extension of the man who does it.

Self-awareness is vital, a knowledge of one's own neurotic "drive." Consciousness is the highest morality.

The Capacity for the Use of Language

By definition the poet is a master of words. Facility in linguistic expression was mentioned more often than any other characteristic in the assessment of personality. Although this capacity would seem to lie on a different level from the three previous ones, being more of an ability than an enduring personality characteristic, it is really commensurate if properly understood. A special attachment to language, an intensity about words, is closely bound up with the capacity for ordering experience. Involvement with words is a concomitant of, and in part an expression of, the desire to entrap and mold experience. Of course non-poets may have an equally intense love of the world and appreciation of rich experience; the mark of the poet is that his experience is couched in verbal form, so that words are for him truly *the* medium of expression. To the writer, words are living things, and seldom merely instrumental, and the talent which masters them is thereby doing more than

100

training or playing; it is exhibiting a deep personal need:

> *Language is itself nonmaterial, but the poet's success depends on how well he makes it an object. Let the language lead the dance . . . put the self behind.*

> *The poet must have a sense of "the word," must be a word-lover.*

> *Language must fit the subject. One can die of linguistic virtuosity. Words cannot be dissociated from the poetic theme. Yeats: "How can you tell the dancer from the dance?"*

> *Love of words is important, but overfacility takes the tension, the carven quality, out of the poem.*

*The Harmoniously Organized Personality
Versus Imbalance*

The exaltation of a state of harmony, and the idea that this harmony of the faculties underlies imaginative achievement, is a pronounced theme in many of the interviews. Most of its adherents seem to be embracing the classical-humanistic view of the whole man, to whom nothing is alien, whose efforts stem from a sense of balanced interest and well-being. The artist, they say, should be "more normal" than other men, more self-possessed and more keenly aware of his own stability:

> *Imagination stems from harmony.*

> *The poet should be a person of wide interests and normal psychological make-up.*

101

But another view is stressed more frequently: that art originates in tensions, that the fully-integrated person feels no need to be an artist. Its advocates state that a measure of imbalance is at the root of creative effort. Inner conflict, in effect, is regarded as the seed from which poetic growth is possible. Although personality flaws are thus countenanced or even blessed as the *sine qua non* of art, it should be noticed that they are always bound up, for the poet, with the goal of productive artistry. That is, he speaks of them as a spur to something else, to be used for the work at hand. There is no glorifying of illness or imbalance for its own sake. The vocational emphasis is so strong as to suggest that the achievement is worth the price in suffering or interpersonal maladjustment:

> *Is life itself to be sacrificed to discipline in work? If being a poet is determined by certain psychological instabilities, the question is whether these can be turned to fruitful effort and production.*
>
> *There should be an imbalance based on sexual dissatisfaction, so that the poet is "hopped-up" with sexual vitality.*
>
> *No poet can be emotionally mature, or approximate the "adult personality." No itch, no poetry. There must be a conflict, or else just quiet sitting. I've got my conscious pretty well under control, but Jesus, my unconscious!*

The poet provokes his own unconscious, by deliberately exposing himself to the strains of exact expression, and by torturing symbols—the words—to fit reality as well as he is able. Of course he may in addition have neurotic tendencies which antedated his concern with art, but these are not "typical" of artists. Lionel Trilling observes that one cannot single out the artist for psychoanalytic explanation—that if the poet's power stems from neurosis, then so does the lawyer's and scientist's. The process of creative endeavor imposes a series of strains; the successful artist surpasses these strains and utilizes the pain they have engendered in order to produce an art product. All men are exposed to neurotic conflict. The poet intensifies this conflict by delving into his own motives and representing irreconcilables to himself. But the poet who actually writes, and writes well, has by that achievement gained a certain mastery over himself, and over the conflict-filled material of his symbolic fund. Again and again, acute students have stressed the poet's power of *control,* his unique ability to make of his fantasy a socially valuable objective entity:

The . . . poet dreams being awake. He is not possessed by his subject but he has dominion over it.— Charles Lamb

But the difference between a work of art and a dream is precisely this—that the work of art leads us back to the outer reality by taking account of it. —Jacques Barzun

But he [the artist] finds a way of return from this

103

fantasy back to reality; with his special gifts, he moulds his fantasies into a new kind of reality; and men concede them a justification as valuable reflections of actual life.——Freud

Coleridge, Rank, Schneider, Trilling, and many others bring out this crucial argument. Thus the artist is regarded as triumphant over the forces of disintegration, precisely because he produces and in producing creates an aesthetic whole which is the obverse of the neurotic's self-defeatism.[12]

The process of creativity is fraught with dangers to the creative personality. It requires of its practitioners a greater strength and sensitivity than most men possess.

[12] Then as th' earth's inward narrow crooked
       lanes
    Do purge sea water's fretful salt away
      I thought, if I could draw my paines
    Through Rime's vexation, I should them allay.
    Griefe brought to numbers cannot be so fierce,
    For, he tames it, that fetters it in verse.
                    ——John Donne, "The Triple Foole"

Aside from the "imperatives" of (1) vitality and integrative force, (2) capacity for association and dissociation, (3) sensitivity, and (4) desire for form and explication, the major theories have been concerned with the conscious-unconscious dialectic and the mechanisms for artistic control of unconscious material. The most general statement would seem to be that creative activity involves

104

the whole man, that all facets of personality come into play, and that the integration of these facets in a constructive task is the problem of the artist as it is the problem of every man. However, the artist embodies his integrative working-through in a traditionally valued vehicle: the work of art. What sets him apart from other men is not a peculiar personality structure inseparable from creativity as such, but the fact of his being "in process" so much more fully and emerging with a concrete result.

The Poet in Society

All that we call sacred history attests that the birth of a Poet is the principal event in chronology.

—Ralph Waldo Emerson

But we must remain firm in our conviction that hymns to the gods and praises of famous men are the only poetry which ought to be admitted into our State. For if you go beyond this and allow the honeyed muse to enter, either in epic or lyric verse, not law and the reason of mankind, which by common consent have ever been deemed best, but pleasure and pain will be the rulers in our State."

—Plato

IF IT IS TRUE that the self is the poet's vocation and that he devotes his major energies to exploring his own personality as a representative focus of human concerns, it is equally true that the poet lives among men in their organized societies. Although we have emphasized the solitary, highly individual nature of the poet's task, one must recognize that even his most private artistic pursuit is not selfish or unique in the usual sense of those words. Rather, the poet tests and refines his perceptions as clues to the most general human responses to the real world of love, dreams, and duties. And he exerts his will toward adequate expression, hence communication, through the marvelously social facility of language. The poet's life among men may be described in several ways, but perhaps the first distinction should be made between his role in the larger society—nation, world, republic of letters—and in the more intimate context of daily face-to-face relations. This chapter will discuss the larger social role, the poet's place in the current American scene, while later chapters involve a more detailed look at selected aspects of his career and his relations to fellow poets.

The poet's role, a vocation on the margin of American society, is unsupported by a framework of conventional patterns to indicate the rewards and responsibilities of practitioners or the demands of the clients. It is an exceptional, personally chosen position which has deep roots in the artistic tradition of Western society but is virtually excluded from the major designs of contemporary occupational or recreational life. Of those who work alone in an American society increasingly dedicated to the abolition of solitude, the poet is perhaps most nearly comparable to the scientific theorist or researcher. But the artist differs sharply from the scientist in that the latter enjoys a fabric of external support and

107

prestige, and works within a limited segment of experience; the scientist is linked to research money, the atomic *mystique,* and the great world of affairs. The number of scientists who actually work alone is also steadily diminishing. Poets, in their roles as verbal innovators, are adventurers in the minds and hearts of men. They have little economic leverage, their names are not well known, and their theater of activity is an intangible universe. The poetic task, always by nature a lonely one, is further aggravated in its isolation by public unconcern and the profusion of stimuli competing for the audience's attention.

Many scholars have supposed that in some era of prehistory all men were artists, or at any rate that each member of society had skills which permitted him to assume the creative role at some time. It has been observed that in contemporary primitive groups the arts are public, not private, and that they serve as "an adornment for public festivity." According to Leach, the various arts tend not to be conceptually separate, and the artist is likely to be at once artist and artisan rather than a professional specialist.

In the modern West, however, the artist's role has typically been specialized and distinct; his separation from other than artistic concerns has been compounded by the rise of expertness and the decline of the "gifted amateur."

Specialization has at least two important consequences. By narrowing but deepening the individual's range

108

of vocational competence, it has sacrificed versatility to a parochial excellence; all the arts thus become in part technical professions, and are set off from the public as things done exceedingly well by experts rather than normal manifestations of an alert, creative spirit. We no longer expect our public men to be occasional writers or painters or patrons, or indeed to have any acquaintance whatever with the arts. To be educated means to master a job, not to cultivate intimate knowledge of a cultural tradition or respond to the varied riches of the general human concern with the arts and sciences. It is not only conceded that a President or cabinet member or corporation executive may be rightly ignorant of poetry, but we would probably think it improper for him to confess such an interest. A second fruit of specialization is the steady chipping away of functions once served by the poet and now largely preëmpted by others whose tasks are more limited. While they cannot seriously be lumped together, a variety of persons including historians, news commentators, television comedians, popular singers, and magazine writers all do some of the things for which poets had formerly been at some juncture responsible. Perhaps the erosion of the poet's role in the United States will only be reversed by the growth of a desire to see the specialized fragments put back together or revealed in a broader spiritual context.

If the role has been specialized, it has also been traditionally arduous and unrewarded. As Sir Arthur Quiller-Couch reminds us:

> The inequity of it is accepted, proverbial,
> and goes back even to legend, to Homer—
> Seven wealthy towns contend for Homer dead
> Through which the living Homer begged his
> bread.

The paucity of recognition enjoyed by most poets during their life-times may of course be related to the fact that the final measure of artistic worth is a matter for posterity, that the poet as prophet may seem much more congenial and valuable to a later age than to his own. Yet it is true that the writer is an exceptional man among non-writers, and that a private excellence may be deprecated as a public excellence is exalted. The poet, after all, has seldom been able to offer anything of immediate public utility. At many times in the past, however, he has appeared to be more closely woven into his society's major patterns of interest and behavior than he is today. Pindar wrote odes to military victory, and Elizabethan playwrights and musicians created for the monarch's pleasure; it is rather difficult to imagine T. S. Eliot celebrating the Battle of Okinawa or Tennessee Williams being commissioned to write a new drama for a Presidential inauguration.

The poet has been an object of suspicion, to be sure. Modern totalitarian regimes have followed Plato's injunction and tried to force conformity to the dogmas of the state. The artist under Communism is perhaps the most pointed example of a situation in which the poet is taken seriously but denied creative freedom. A deadly

110

yet fascinating picture of poetry in the Communist state is given by Czeslaw Milosz:

> Poetry as we have known it can be defined as the individual temperament refracted through social convention. The poetry of the New Faith can, on the contrary, be defined as social convention refracted through the individual temperament.
>
> The New Faith is a Russian creation, and the Russian intelligentsia which shaped it had developed the deepest contempt for all art that does not serve social ends directly. Other social functions of art, probably the most important ones, consistently escaped its understanding. As for poetry, since its sources are hard to differentiate from the sources of all religion, it is singularly exposed to persecution. True, the poet is free to describe hills, trees, and flowers, but if he should feel that boundless exaltation in the face of nature that seized Wordsworth on his visit to Tintern Abbey, he is at once suspect. This is an excellent means of eliminating the legions of bad poets who like to confess their pantheistic flights publicly, but it is also a means of exterminating poetry as a whole and replacing it by jingles little better than the singing commercials broadcast over the radio in America.

This analysis stands in very sharp contrast to the prevailing mood in the United States and other Western democracies. Our American suspicion of the poet, while quite real, is seldom expressed politically. We confront him, not with an iron dictate, but with a sedulous disregard. Yet many have seen pressures toward artistic conformity in the West springing from another source, from society as a vast undiscriminating public rather than from the state as patron. The disappearance of royal and aristocratic patronage, coupled with the flourishing mass media of communication, left the poet in a market situation. Since the market was theoretically composed of all readers, most of whom wished to be comfortably entertained rather than challenged by literary excellence, economic survival might involve pandering to popular taste rather than striving for poetic value.[1] Thus in eighteenth-century England one finds a Goldsmith or Fielding worrying about artistic integrity in the mass market, a problem which was still unresolved for Ezra Pound, who complained in twentieth-century America that ·the demand for slick magazine verse meant a levelling and lowering of saleable poetry.

The mass audience and its capricious tastes, matched with growing emphasis on mercantile values and conventional bourgeois morality, seems to have inspired the romantic stereotype of the alienated writer. In the past

---

[1] See, for instance, Leo Lowenthal and Marjorie Fiske: "Reaction to Mass Media Growth in 18th-Century England," *Journalism Quarterly*, XXXIII, Fall, 1956.

century and a half, it has become fashionable to speak
of the artist *versus* society as if there were an inevitable
opposition between the creator and his social environment. It is significant that the writer enunciated the
enmity; there are few instances of frontal attack on the
artistic role by government officials, businessmen, or anyone else. Whatever its justification in the past or its
relevance to the condition of today's American poet, the
idea of the writer at odds with society is an important
part of our cultural tradition. An amusing comment
which fixes the idea properly in its literary origins is
given by Donald Barr in his review of Joyce Cary's
novel, *The Horse's Mouth:*

> "The Horse's Mouth" is the autobiography of
> Gulley Jimson. Gulley is our old friend the
> artist at odds with society. Novels are full of
> painters and musicians and poets, and they are
> always at odds with society. And how gloomy
> and embarrassed about it they are! But Gulley,
> the bald, little, bandy-legged swaggerer humbly
> dedicated to art, meticulously painting The Fall
> of Man with the frayed stub of a rope and some
> stolen colors, threatening to cut the tripe out
> of a millionaire, forging his own works, and
> grandly blocking out his last huge masterpiece
> on a crumbling wall—Gulley is at odds with
> society in a new way, in dozens of new ways.
> Society hasn't a chance. This fellow enjoys
> being an artist.

113

Baudelaire and Gulley Jimson may be set at opposite poles among artists in revolt. In contemporary America the poet no longer seems bound to consider himself an enemy of society, but if he does his general attitude is perhaps spiritually closer to Gulley's buoyant aggression than to the bitter disenchantment professed by a Baudelaire or Rimbaud.

Baudelaire's is the classic statement of the poet's feeling that he is hounded by an unsympathetic social environment:

> If a poet asked the state for permission to keep a few bourgeois in his stable everyone would be greatly astonished; but if a bourgeois asked for some roast poet, it would be considered perfectly natural.

The case of the poet in American society is especially interesting because the very trends toward a mechanical and bureaucratic life which repelled European artists have here reached most acute form. It is generally accepted that the colonial and post-Revolutionary periods in the United States failed to produce artists of the first rank. Citizens of that age were presumably much too busy staking out a new republic and battling their physical environment to devote much attention to the arts. Most of the productions of that and immediately succeeding periods were either too clumsy to merit critical consideration or too derivative of English models to stand as truly American literature. We note then (de Tocque-

114

ville) as in the later nineteenth century (Henry Adams) the primary antithesis between a pragmatic penchant for getting things done fast and efficiently and a firm resolve to get things done beautifully if slowly.

Most critics point to the mid-nineteenth century as the years of artistic intensity in America. The Concord group, and other figures in F. O. Mathiesson's "American Renaissance," stand for the heights of literary fruition. The names of Melville, Poe, Emily Dickinson, Walt Whitman, Emerson, Thoreau, are taken as climactic. Of the poets, it is Poe, Whitman, and Dickinson who are singled out for special praise as the progenitors of native verse.

Matthew Josephson develops the thesis that after this golden day the serious writer became progressively alienated in spirit from the main course of American life. Of course he can point to non-recognition and marginal status of the artist even before the late 1800's. But it is in the booty stage of American capitalism, the post-Civil War expansion of railroads and industry, that he finds the locus of disenchantment. The mercantile emphasis, the stress on unaesthetic utility, the lack of public response, all contrived to produce in the artist a feeling of separation from society. Josephson assumes that this society rejected the artist; if the public indeed did so implicitly, certain it is that the artist proclaimed an explicit rejection of his country. The exiles went the length to physical rejection, as in the expatriation of Henry James, of Whistler, of Eliot and Pound in the early twentieth century. The stay-at-homes were in many cases unhappy with their lot. Recall Melville's, "I feel I am an exile here." The individual who stayed in America seemed doomed to eccentricity: "The fatalistic, the silenced Melville, the outcast Whitman, the mysteriously secluded Emily Dickinson." What reasons are adduced for this situation, which may err on the gloomy side but is nevertheless a largely correct summary of what writers felt their lot to be? Levelling and standardization of values, and mechanization of life are most often put forth as antecedents of artistic discontent:

> The artist, then, appears most vulnerable. In a society become increasingly collective and uniform in its interests, no place has been left for his lonely and personal labors. With such a world art in the older sense can no longer co-exist.

> Under mechanism, the eternal drama for the artist becomes resistance to the milieu, as if the highest prerogative were the preservation of the individual type, the defense of the human self from dissolution in the horde.

In this dilemma the poet represents one of the critical questions of contemporary Western civilization. Simmel stated the problem in general terms:

> The deepest problems of modern life derive from the claim of the individual to preserve the autonomy and individuality of his existence in the face of overwhelming social forces, of histori-

116

cal heritage, of external culture, and of the technique of life.

To balance the picture of the artist as a social isolate of ignoble status, we may think of the "Indian Summer" of New England, of Chautauqua with its idolatry of "culture," of the general (and genteel) fashionableness of literary activity. Yet the critics affirm that those artists of sterner vein, who were to be recognized as giants by a later generation, were for the most part badly treated. So Dahlberg weeps for Melville buried in a poor grave:

> Is it not fitting, so American, that the most astonishing genius that ever came out of the Western hemisphere, should be so uncleanly slabbed down in mean cheap dirt not among the pitiable poor but with the common drab bulk of rightly unremembered dead. Look upon his homely sparse tombstone and read the frugal inscription written thereon, "Occupation, "Writer," and then utter aloud the pity for the artist, in America, alive or deceased, it matters not, that Hamlet so dolorously sighs forth before his father's apparition, "Alas! Poor Ghost."

In 1913, we find Ezra Pound the possessor of a somewhat brighter view, although it is still weighted toward the dark themes of isolation and rejection. For Pound, while stating in definite terms the obstacles to poetry in this country, had hope of a development toward better days: "I have declared my belief in the imminence of an

117

American Risorgimento. I have no desire to flatter the country by pretending that we are at present enduring anything except the Dark Ages." He sets up American vigor and "clumsy energy" against the flowering of the arts, noting that politics and business drain talented individuals away from the artist role. Of the Americans he said in *"Patria Mia"*:

> One knows that they are the dominant people and that they are against all delicate things. They will never imagine beautiful plaisaunces. They will never "sit on a midden and dream stars," as the Irish peasant said to Joseph Campbell.

The status of the American poet today is difficult to describe, for it is an ambiguous and various complex of attitudes and values. While some forsee a general raising of artist and intellectual in the public eye, stimulated by increased literacy and leisure, it is apparent that the poet's craft is far from the concerns of most members of American society. In one sense his position is bettered by the wide influence of poets and critics in academic circles, and a resulting increase in intelligent interest. Public readings of poetry have drawn large audiences, recordings by poets are stocked in libraries, and one poet a year has been formally recognized by the Library of Congress as Consultant in Poetry. Yet it would be false to suppose that the appellation poet evokes an unusually affirmative response from the mass of Americans, or that it implies any great respect. He is no culture hero, but is probably more nearly disregarded than disvalued in any explicit sense. A *lack* of attribution of high status is not the same as the attribution of low status, for broadly speaking the poet is not scorned but neglected. His role is simply not in the public ken, and this despite a healthy, important production of poetry in modern America. Many leading observers, in fact, emphasize that the writing of contemporary and recent native poets is of extremely good quality, a true growth of poetic tradition matching other high points in aesthetic history.

In *Poets at Work* Auden sums up the mixed, uncomfortable status of most poets today:

> Everyone in his heart of hearts agrees with Baudelaire: 'to be a useful person has always seemed to me something particularly horrible,' for, subjectively, to be useful means to be doing not what one wants to do but what someone else insists on one's doing. But at the same time, everyone is ashamed to admit in public that he is useless. Thus if a poet gets into conversation with a stranger in a railway coach and the latter asks him: "What is your job?," he will think quickly and say: 'A school-teacher, a beekeeper, a bootlegger', because to tell the truth would cause an incredulous and embarrassing silence.

Why should the artist, the specialist in symbolic

119

creativity, enjoy a tenuous position in American society? He originates form and content which afford pleasure and more than pleasure, the rich insights and stark perceptions to make experience meaningful. Yet he can seldom earn a living in his vocation, seldom count on any broadly based support in his chosen role; he must be as ready for depreciation as for appreciation, and this according to criteria seemingly remote from consideration of artistic excellence. If we analyze the poet's work and life in the context of American values, it may be possible to understand his frail roots in our cultural soil. It should be stressed, however, that American society only accentuates the traditionally precarious role of the artistic innovator. In nearly every place and time the truly creative individual has represented a threat to the norms men live by, since he promises to shatter or transcend or at least drastically to amend those norms. The creative individual in art is the more dangerous because he challenges our ways of perceiving and our habits of expressing what we see. Unlike the political revolutionary or social reformer, who would change the forms of social intercourse, the artist would change our emotional response to the universe of man and nature. In this he is like the scientist revising our rational perceptions or the religious leader enhancing our moral perceptions.

The texture of American culture is so rich and complicated that generalizations about specific themes of value and behavior are always hazardous. For every statement that this or that pattern is dominant or recessive, one can easily adduce contrary evidence. Although an analyst must arbitrarily break through the almost oppressive heterogeneity of social forms, it is well to begin by recognizing that pluralism is itself perhaps the most prominent theme. Pluralism of values is in fact a chief support of the artist, in that it lets him work out a unique destiny of vocational fulfillment. While it is true that cultural diversity may make communication more difficult, reducing the scope of any single shared tradition or contemporary frame of reference, diversity also provides the poet with a range of alternative life styles, economically rewarding pursuits other than poetry, and several potential kinds of audience. Again, the habit of tolerance in religious and political matters tends to insure the tolerance of artistic heresy. If we let artists die of neglect it can scarcely be said that we hound them with demands for conformity to any particular doctrine of state or ideology. Our disinterested tolerance itself, however, has been seen by Milosz as a very mixed blessing:

> Fear of the indifference with which the economic system of the West treats its artists and scholars is widespread among Eastern intellectuals. They say it is better to deal with an intelligent devil than with a good-natured idiot. An intelligent devil understands their mutual interests and lets them live by a pen, a chisel, or a brush, caring for his clients and making his demands. A good-hearted idiot does not under-

121

stand these interests, gives nothing and asks nothing—which in practice amounts to polite cruelty.

Underlying the pluralism of tradition there are a few clusters of prominent American themes against which the artist may be viewed.

The Protestant Ethic and the Spirit of Poetry

The Protestant ethic as described, for instance, by Max Weber, is in a very fundamental sense antipathetic to poetry. This is true despite the high rank of the greatest Puritan poet, Milton, and despite certain superficial similarities between the Calvinist ethical ideal and that of the artist-as-ascetic. While the concept of the "calling," of devotion to a disciplined activity, is very relevant to poetic dedication, the context of the poet's calling is singular. For his work by its very nature demands a breadth of enjoyment, a love of the pleasures of this world, which is foreign to "duty capitalism." The Protestant ethic, like the utilitarian doctrine, emphasizes the extrinsic goals of vocational struggle: heavenly residence and profits are alike in their displacement from the work activity itself. Weber has shown how the goal of election into a celestial state of grace became subordinated, in the later development of Calvinist-inspired work ethics, to the idea that work is good for its own sake. Yet this Calvinist work is not the poet's work, since it is not to be enjoyed but nobly endured. Obviously an entrepreneur could not legitimately derive

122

pleasure from a calling which had been imposed as dutiful striving.

The poet is too apparently a man who derives pleasure from his task, and that pleasure is a sensuous one. The immediacy of creative work implies acceptance and deep enjoyment of emotional nuances. The poet plays with words and loves them for their own sweet verbal sakes; he is stimulated by his own productions. The Protestant ethic, rightly learned, involves a positive distaste for pleasure, and especially for sensuous pleasure. We might parody Macaulay's famous remark about the Puritans and bear-baiting by noting that American society rejects the poet, not because of the pain (or ease) he gives his readers, but because of the pleasure he obviously gets from writing, and the personal talent he exhibits. It is furthermore a peculiar feature of the artist's work that he rarely appears, to a casual observer, to be working at all. Actual writing is known to consume a rather small portion of the writer's day, even when he is in high gear. And there are periods, well described by E. D. Hutchinson as "Periods of Renunciation" in creative endeavor, when nothing happens to be going just right, no new idea has jelled, and the artist must stick it out. The "sticking it out" may take the form of loafing; although everyone agrees that a certain kind of loafing is crucial to any intellectually creative activity, it still seems to the public not quite right or wholly just. The public, as Bergler notes, envies the writer while scorning him for his apparent ease. In a country where

123

occupational life is characterized by intense "busy work" and routine, the person of no fixed outer demands is looked upon somewhat askance. This occurs despite the fact that there may be inner personal demands, in poet or scientist, more strict than anything the time clock or straw boss imposes.

Routine and Originality

In modern Western society, occupations are very generally molded into systems of routine. The complexity of huge bureaucratic-industrial organizations demands that the specific task assigned through division of labor be subject to precise planning. The typical job should be geared to explicit standards of performance, technique, and interrelation with other closely allied functions. Not only is the job itself systematically defined, but the training that fits an individual for the position is specified and clearly established to fit the goal of competent performance. All of this ordering and accountability means further that the vast majority of occupations are institutionalized; that is, the activities involved in carrying them out are well-understood and predictable by all the parties to the situation. Performance of certain roles is an accepted feature of the social system, and both the performers and the people importantly related to them know what is legitimately to be expected. The "public" has too a disposition to regard as justified an activity for which formal social provision is made, which can be objectively "certified." Few of

124

these strictures apply significantly to poetry as a profession. It is true that strict standards of competence are applied by literary critics, but even here the criteria are amorphous. Writing is a sedentary and private activity; the poet grows no callouses, goes to no offices, punches no time clock, gains no diploma, earns no certificate of competence. There is no current, universal measure of his success or fitness; his credentials are intangible, a passport without date, country, or occupation. Poetry is an "undefined" profession. It lacks either the institutional support or the popular magical appeal of science, with which it is alone comparable in terms of originality of contribution.

The Poetic Role and the "Revolt of the Masses"

Ortega y Gassett has analyzed the tremendous power of the "mass man." He sees the rise to dominance of the great bulk of average individuals, through the democratic franchise and the weakening of older social hierarchies, as the primary fact of our times. Nowhere is the phenomenon more fully exemplified than in the United States. That this should result in a vast pressure toward conformity and mediocrity is not surprising. De Tocqueville made careful note of "levelling" tendencies in America over a century ago. Perhaps genius and talent are always suspect; one doubts that physicists are wholly accepted in this country, despite the practical efficacy of the atomic bomb. Mass dominance implies a standardization of values, and a distrust of the unique. These

125

tendencies are accentuated enormously by the media of mass communication, which insure that the value standard becomes a common denominator. The common denominator is not necessarily "low" for being common; it may be quite high, as exemplified in the very real increase of interest in classical music, but it *is* axiomatically weighted toward uniformity.

The poet is by definition the teller of a personal truth. He is unique and abides by an uncommon denominator. As a minority of one, he falls under many of the strains imposed on other, more obtrusive minorities.

Pragmatism and Poetry

Americans do things, and go places. The poet does things and goes places too, but he does unusual things and goes to uncharted places. This in itself makes him suspect. But he is guilty of a worse crime, and one that sets his role more incontrovertibly against the American temper: his efforts have no obvious utility. In this respect he is more deviant than the gangster, whose activities are at least useful to himself in that they may make him rich before they get him killed or imprisoned. The molder of aesthetic symbols may reform the language, transmute and communicate experience, delight the reader with originality of form. But, the popular pragmatist might ask, to what end are these things done? We accept the notion of "pure research" in the sciences because we have learned by experience that such efforts often result in efficacious and profitable by-products.

The poet does pure research in the human heart, but few Americans could be convinced that his work compares in importance with that of a specialist on coronary thrombosis.

The Artist's Role and the Feminine Role

In American culture generally, women have been the carriers of the arts. They have not often been of the first rank artistically or critically, but overall they have borne the burden of aesthetic proof. In a very real sense, American males have delegated to their wives, and even more definitely to women of the old-maid-schoolteacher stereotype, the responsibility for what is popularly known as "culture." A superficial explanation of this phenomenon might point to the frontier imperatives, which later became the business imperatives, of energetic effort, devotion to external detail, and resolute "toughness" on the part of the male. As Erikson has so beautifully shown, one of the duties of the mother in this country has been to push the son firmly in the direction of untrammeled maleness and striving, meanwhile sedulously smothering the child's impulse for things sensual and immediate. This emphasis, if firmly pursued, would seem to leave poetry to women or to males who rebel against so confining a model of attitude and action.

Yet this is not the whole story. When Carol Kennicott tried to bring the arts to Gopher Prairie, and we note that this is a typically womanish project, she was met by more than a plain refusal to be concerned; she was met in fact by positive male hostility. Why should American men avoid the artist's calling and tend to deprecate those who follow it?

We may suggest that, going deeper than the female's history as the functional art-bearer in the American tradition, there are elements intrinsic to the roles of male and female which militate against men-as-artists. What has been called the American man's "panic fear of homosexuality" may be relevant to the ambiguous position of the male poet. As the Kluckhohns and others have stressed, it is comparatively easy for men to be "scared" out of being artists. A major basis for this fear may be found in the observation that the general emotional responsiveness which characterizes the feminine role as outlined, for example, by Parsons, is also quite typical of the artist role. In this connection, Parsons has remarked upon the revealing use of the term "longhair," usually in a derogatory vein, to describe artists and their works. May it not be a dramatic symbol of the hostility often directed against the artist who oversteps arbitrary distinctions between sex roles? This correspondence of themes suggests that the fear and hostility the poet often meets are contingent on his not consistently "acting like a man" in conventional terms. The poet incorporates too much, refuses to be bound by criteria of typical social behavior, and exhibits an "unmasculine" concern with senses and sensitivity.

Related to the artist's greater *capacity* for experience is the possibility that his learning, his stock of impressions and responses, is too huge for him to fit easily into a restricted sex role. Thus he takes in elements of both male and female roles, as do all men, but then refuses to forsake "feminine" qualities and capacities at a later statge. Perhaps he never succeeds in unlearning the infant's play impulses or warmly sensuous responses to the world. One might propose, then, that the artist role and the feminine role are intimately related—often to the social detriment of the artist—not because artists are constitutionally "queer" but because our culture demands a distinction between roles on the thematic, learned level which the artist is unable or unwilling to meet. Unable to smother his emotional resonance and widely inclusive responses to life in favor of the more "strict" male occupational model, the poet finds himself too versatile in a specialized world. As "the apple tree, the singing and the gold" do not promote the world's work, so they do not provide a wholly acceptable pattern of male activity in contemporary American life.

The Ideal of Self-Fulfillment

The American belief in an individual, self-determined destiny that will express the essential talents of each person is one of the strongest props for unusual vocations. The idea that one's social role, far from being predetermined by accidents of birth or environment, represents the choice made by a relatively free agent implies the right to choose odd styles of life and seemingly incomprehensible goals. Despite the very real pressures toward

conformity, and especially toward a success measured by
material gain, there is a range of tolerance for the artist
who is doing the kind of thing that appeals to him. The
shocked disbelief that greets the announcement that
one's son has turned to poetry or painting is not un-
mixed with respectful envy, an admiration however
grudging for the individual who hews to his own path.
The spate of popular volumes which preach self-fulfillment and personal development attests to the American
taste for free self-expression as well as the need for reiterating the ideal in a society which seems to force many
people into roles they might not choose again as free
agents. It is true that the notion of an individual's "doing what he wants to do" is usually implicitly qualified
by the criteria of financial gain, but one must attach
great importance to the fact that parents in this society
feel guilty about pushing their children into uncongenial
vocations. So a way is left open for the artist, who represents a pure type of self-fulfillment. There can be little
doubt that of all men the poet is most concerned with
the burgeoning of his own personality, his sensitivity
and perceptivity. It is after all his only stock in trade,
the only instrument he will ever have to perform mir-
acles of words. The dramatic moment when Sherwood
Anderson walked out of his paint factory and family
and routine set of social roles to become a professional
writer is perhaps a symbol for the right of self-expression. Today it is debatable whether an aspiring novelist
would even have to walk out of the factory or out of his

130

settled life style; he might be encouraged in his native circumstances to the point where flight was meaningless.

Education and Leisure

Americans now have the highest general level of education and the most leisure time ever enjoyed by a society as a whole. The effect of this situation on the arts and the artist is not yet clear, but it will undoubtedly change the artist's role by transforming the nature of the audience. More people now have the humanistic acquaintance which is necessary to make the arts individually meaningful, and they have free time to read or visit museums or listen to concerts. Respect for the professional artist may increase as more amateurs try to master the techniques of painting and writing. The tiny leisure class which has traditionally provided aristocratic patrons is being expanded in this country toward a kind of classless leisure, a potential source of broad support for artistic activities. It is certainly conceivable that creation and recreation may tend to merge if the mass media do not succeed in consuming all of everyone's spare hours. The great world of events piped to our living rooms may come to be too much with us, so that the private world of one poet and one reader becomes an attractive sanctuary.

Although we have seen that American values in their variety both harbor and reject the poet, it is obvious that his work diverges rather sharply from the vocational paths which men in this society are expected to follow.

In part the divergence is negative, consisting of his not embracing certain common goals such as economic gain or social position and not employing certain common means such as professional training or climbing the rungs of a large organization. These negative elements are the core of the idea that the artist is a deviant person, but they do not lead us very far because in these terms the poet is indistinguishable from the hobo or the psychotic. The really important questions arise when one asks what the artist puts in place of the behaviors he has rejected.

The poet as maker rejects the conventional perceptions of the world of men and nature. His implicit goal is to make his reader more aware of the complexity and ambiguity of existence, not by preaching but by vigorous example of fresh ways of seeing. The artist forces us to give up, at least momentarily, those routine, comfortable stereotypes on which we depend to keep the world under safe control. This is why full participation in aesthetic experience may be nearly as psychologically threatening for the appreciator as for the creator. The threat, like almost all challenges to an established system of behavior (for example, neurosis) has as much potential for growth and refreshment as for confusion or debilitation. Yet we naturally resist the challenge to follow the poet into novel modes of reacting to experience and novel words for expressing that reaction. It not only bestirs us, since art may in one sense be seen as the opposite of a state of rest, but it also confronts us with the imperative to grow, to enlarge our own perceptions enough to entertain some part of the artist's perceptions.

Because the heightening of awareness is an endless occupation, halting only with death or complete un-awareness, the poet cannot be said to have a "goal" in the usual sense. His essential goal is more of the same, renewed involvement in the process of living and writing. It is true that he wants to achieve the perfect line, the absolute phrase; but this is an intangible end, really the prelude to the next perfect line, and it is so elusive that many writers would agree with the aphorism that, "a poem is never finished, it is abandoned in despair." If the artist's goal is difficult to define, and tends to be a process rather than a static accomplishment, what can one say about his means? They are so extraordinary, when compared with the instrumental maneuvers of most individuals in society, that the question of "how he does it" may put the poet further from the dominant patterns of behavior than the question of "why does he do it?" In large part, his means is simply to live as fully and sensitively as possible, to be a mobile perceptual antenna at the boundary of human consciousness. Be-cause he spends so much of his time doing precisely this, he may be and often is accused of being a non-contrib-uting member of society. When he comes to the actual job of writing, he performs in a private world. Only when some reader happens to receive his gift and enter to a certain degree the universe of cognition and emo-tion he has elaborated, does the poet come to have an obvious social function.

As the creator of expressive symbols, the artist eventually has an effect. It is likely to be a slow and subtle one, like that of the religious leader, the philosopher, or the scientist, for it consists in changing the basic views of men and reforming the tongue they use to express those views. We then face an interesting problem: the very innovators whose transcendence of common values has in the long run the most highly valued effect are treated as marginal men in the contemporary social scheme. Many reasons may be adduced for this treatment, including the uncomfortable wrench the artist gives to conventional ways of seeing, and the time lag between what the artist does and what his potential publics may grow to accept. Fewer good reasons may be found, however, for the failure of social scientists to devote adequate attention to the exceptional person, the creative individual in whatever sphere. Social theorists have tended uncritically to accept the premises of their own cultural framework to the extent of dividing people into those who follow conventional social prescriptions closely and those whose refusal to follow them results in deleterious—criminal or ill—behavior. They have neglected to consider the talented person who surmounts inherited patterns in search of something better or fuller. Psychologists too, as Allport has recently maintained, have been bound to a model of man as reactive organism, who could be seen as responding to external stimuli (therefore capable of accepting or rejecting sensations, including social norms) but not as initiating creative activity (therefore capable of devising new values and refining old ones).

134

Since the creative individual is demonstrably important in society, we need a sophisticated view of innovative behavior. Such a view is required both for what might be termed *institutionalized* innovation, as in science, and for the singular creativity that occurs in less systematic spheres, as in art and religion. Some clues exist, in such diverse contexts as Max Weber's concept of *charisma* (creative leadership), psychoanalytic studies of the origins of artistic behavior, and current research into the personality characteristics of talented individuals. But a true social psychology of creativity must be grounded in a series of detailed investigations, embracing everything from childhood development to the style of life of the mature innovator. As Henry A. Murray has expressed it, the sociologist must turn from an exclusive preoccupation with "associational" roles which are defined by obvious patterns of social relationships toward some cognizance of "monadic" or individually creative roles. The problem of analyzing the role of the artist or scientist is not an exotic or peripheral one merely because their behaviors are complicated and they are a numerically tiny segment of the population. The poet and the physicist are not only highly significant in their society, but in their vocational paths they raise the major issues for the student of man: conformity and social control, the relation of the individual to his various social groupings, the creation of percepts and values by which the social fabric is torn or mended or graven with bold new designs.

The Poetic Career

CHAPTER V

As things are, and as fundamentally they must
always be, poetry is not a career but a mug's
game. No honest poet can ever feel quite sure
of the permanent value of what he has written:
he may have wasted his time and messed up his
life for nothing.

—T. S. Eliot

POETIC CAREERS are as various as poets themselves, which
is to say that no firm line of the typical poet's progress
can be laid down. The absence of any well-defined route
to mature artistic activity may be traced, in part, to the
paucity of external guideposts for the aspiring poet in
American society, of agreed-upon techniques for the
writer's nurture and support. We have no established
network of patronage or apprenticeship, and except for
academic jobs no tradition of occupational "cushions"
such as the British civil service, for instance, has sometimes provided for writers. Underlying this vacuum in
which the young poet must make his way is the general

lack of public concern with poetry and the familiar parental disinclination to launch children on a career which promises little in the way of fame or money. But young men and women persist in venting the poetic impulse, and a few of them follow this impulse into a life-long affair with the muse. How do they become poets, and what sustains them in this hardy enterprise—so hardy, indeed, that modern poets, far from being "soft" aesthetes, tend to be exceedingly tough-minded citizens?

Poets are neither born nor made, since native talent or schooled facility, taken singly, are each insufficient to inspire true art. The gifts of seeing and speaking freshly do not lead to poetry if they are not accompanied by a controlled technique, and the most refined metrical or verbal mastery is incomplete without original vision. The poetic career is, rather, a composite of early desire, tutored experience, and infinite rehearsal. Most poets credit literature itself as the first and most profound influence on their vocational choice. They read poetry, enjoy it, and develop a need to go and do likewise. When poets speak of childhood exposure to poetry, they use the language of delighted discovery, a tongue charged with emotion despite its abuse on Madison Avenue: astonishment, amazement, surprise, joy, enchantment. It is as if they were finding for the first time that the prosaic world of parents, of normal childhood initiation, opens onto another world of wider landscapes and intuitive celebrations. They respond to the joy and freedom of verse by reading more and more of it, until the poet's

137

world becomes a favored ground, familiar yet hallowed. And it should be remarked that the young person's immersion in literature is not an escape from life. The idea that reading is an alternative to something "more real" is one of the more pernicious untruths in American culture; properly seen, of course, the zest for reading is a zest for new experience, an abundant reaching-out which is psychologically contrary to retreat.

The poet tends to be an early bloomer, to begin acting like a poet—and often showing marks of a distinct talent —at a relatively early age. Yet whether the serious involvement in the career is early or late, and whether the choice is deliberate or a concession to an accomplished fact, literature remains the primary source of inspiration. The poetic tradition has the power to attract its own neophytes: poetry breeds poets. Dr. Johnson gives an admirable example in his life of Abraham Cowley:

> In the window of his mother's apartment lay Spenser's Fairy Queen; in which he very early took delight to read, till by feeling the charms of verse, he became, as he relates, irrecoverably a poet. Such are the accidents which, sometimes remembered, and perhaps sometimes forgotten, produce that particular designation of mind, and propensity for some certain science or employment, which is commonly called Genius.

Perhaps the most frequent impetus to the career occurs in just this way, so that the talented individual loving poetry becomes "irrecoverably a poet." Instead

138

of sitting down and consciously picking poetry as a vocation, the person grows into it by a subtle yet steady
process. Contemporary American poets seldom look back
on a single determined occupational choice. One who
does, however, testifies to the literary influence:

> *I have never wanted to be anything else. At the
> age of nine, I read* Tom Brown's Schooldays, *which
> had an introduction containing two lines of verse:*
> > *I'm the poet of White Horse vale, sir,*
> > *With liberal notions under my cap.*
> *I asked my parents what a poet was, and when they
> told me I was fascinated. I went to school and saw
> several words listed on the board; I made a rhyme
> scheme, and this was my first poem. I always knew
> I would be a poet.*

Even those who came to poetry somewhat later in
life tend to stress the importance of literary stimuli:

> *It was not deliberate, and was based on the plea-
> sure principle. I read modern poems in high school,
> not dreaming that I could write one. Then one day
> I wrote one, loved the experience and wanted to
> repeat it.*

> *The exposure to literature is important; poetic
> activity must spring from somewhere. I wrote some
> poetry in college, but was not very involved with it.
> I wrote much prose, and becoming dissatisfied with
> it, turned to poetry.*

The power of the poetic tradition is of course rein-

139

forced by the presence of some few mentors and colleagues, themselves sharers of the verbal heritage and
partners in the creative enterprise. An older colleague
will often call one's work to the attention of editor or
publisher. Ezra Pound's reputation in literary circles
is actually based quite as much on his letters and encouraging overtures to young poets as on his own artistic
contribution; many older writers feel that the nurture
of young talent is a duty imposed on the established person, although it is to be sure a duty of enthusiasm rather
than compulsion. Contemporary poets are vividly aware
of influential figures:

> *I had to quit athletics because of my health. After
> trying all the arts, I fixed on poetry. I met "X" at
> the university. He was a major influence on me,
> giving me good freshman literary criticism, not
> vague but in clear declarative sentences.*
>
> *I firmly settled on poetry while at Cambridge,
> largely under the influence of I. A. Richards and
> William Empson.*
>
> *What I need most is someone to fight like hell
> with. Women are to go to bed with, men are to fight
> with. My association with Ezra Pound helped inspire
> me to continue writing poetry. For years we waged a
> battle over the proper goal of the poet; I would say,
> "bread" and Pound would say, "caviar."*

One may then sum up the early phases of the career,
in the United States today, by emphasizing the double

140

influence of literary example and informal tutelage by older poets, critics, and teachers. A good deal of luck is implied by the haphazard character of the latter influence; a young poet may or may not find an interested teacher, a sympathetic editor, or a congenial colleague. There is no doubt that certain aspects of the craft may be taught, both by example and by close criticism of the younger poet's ongoing work. Perhaps even more important than technical guidance is the quality of encouragement offered by an established person who cares deeply. The master-apprentice relationship may take many forms, ranging from an almost parental concern to a cold schooling. It is apt to be ridden with tensions, of which the most obvious are artistic jealousy of master for student, and a demand by one or both parties for the exclusive loyalty and attention of the other. There is an opportunity, especially with respect to first publication, for the older figure to exert a certain leverage in extra-poetic affairs, such as making the apprentice a sexual partner or restricting his range of friendships. But these are ancient and well-known stresses for the artistic neophyte.

Finally, the inner drive toward poetic innovation appears to many artists as a "given," an historical personal fact which must somehow be accommodated and woven into one's style of life:

> It was an accidental, not a conscious, decision.
> But I felt a lack when I was doing something else,
> as if I were not using myself.

141

*You're generally a poet because you have to be,
not because you decide you want to be.*

*In this art, in distinction from painting, one must
begin early. There is the necessity of much practice,
so that one achieves technical mastery before the
finding of his individual voice. Poetry is always
there. If it is with you, you will make a place for it.*

The poetic career grows with and on the individual
in such a way that he ordinarily becomes enmeshed in it
without making a formal decision. Poetry, springing
from within, flourishes despite the very amorphous and
unregulated nature of the career pattern. The task is
one of process—to *write* poetry—rather than one of
offices and perquisites—to *be* a poet. An aspirant who
thirsts for worldly goals in the vein of conventional
American success, for a certain income or reputation, is
not only ordained for disappointment; his very striving,
if it takes precedence over the hard work of art itself,
will be generally scorned by his peers.[1]

It would be a mistake to assume that a career in
poetry is always determined solely by an inner longing
that makes the vocational path inevitable. Dr. Johnson
speaks of the "accidents" that shape the course of genius,
and American poets too reflect the influence of fortuitous

---

[1] See, for instance, Dylan Thomas's delightfully vitri-
olic essay, "How To Be A Poet," *Atlantic Monthly,*
July, 1951.

events. No one can say that a certain individual would not have become a poet without some particular juncture of circumstances, yet historical accidents are frequently cited. One man was headed for a business career when the family fortune was lost; he sailed around the world to reexamine his life, and, forced into acute awareness by the depression of the thirties, turned back to the poetry he had merely dabbled with in college. Again, a woman found early success in the theater, but when her dramatic company disbanded she returned to the poetry which had always been a background theme in her life.

The pursuit of poetry involves deep pleasures: the satisfaction of a personal need and the conviction that one is living fully, using the self to capacity for a more than selfish purpose. Playful work and serious play, it is the noble word game in which one gambles for the very highest stakes of self-discovery and artistic mastery. The career today, however, entails a series of renunciations which are the more binding as the individual approaches total commitment to his art. Of these the most critical is money, since with very few exceptions poets cannot actually earn a living by selling their verse. Putting aside the question of high income or genuine enrichment, which is clearly irrelevant in the poet's context, there is still the problem of a minimum income to sustain civilized existence. In nearly all cases, therefore, the poet must have a double vocation: his poetry and some other activity which is financially rewarding.

A job which will pay and still fit into the writer's pattern of life is a prime requirement for the poetic career. How the two vocations are to be woven together, when one of them—poetry—demands high energy and zealous attention, is thus an issue of first importance for the serious poet in the United States.

The other major focus of renunciation centers around the lack of recognition and encouragement on any appreciable scale. Probably all men want to think their jobs important, to receive prestige for doing them well, to be offered spiritual support by interested persons. Poets, even if they are keenly self-rewarded and secure in the knowledge of their own intrinsic worth, cannot thrive in a vacuum. If a broad audience and a reasonable measure of social prestige are unavailable to the individual in his role as poet, then he must look to some more unique and special outer support.

Malcolm Cowley once challenged the axiom that no one can make a living by writing poetry in the United States by remarking that as yet he knew of no poet who had really tried. We may recall that Milton counseled the tragic poet to drink plain water from a wooden bowl, and that the artist-as-ascetic has always been expected to keep his wants modest. At any rate, the income of at best a few hundred dollars from a book of verse is not enough to sustain life; perhaps the only poets who could now live on royalties are the handful of international figures at late stages in their careers like Robert Frost or T. S. Eliot.

144

A book of poems returns its author a maximum of fifteen percent per copy, or thirty cents on a two-dollar book. Such volumes usually "sell" somewhat less than a thousand copies. Since few poets produce more than one book a year, royalty income is obviously almost negligible. Publication is hard to achieve, especially for younger poets, so that even this tiny reward is by no means guaranteed. Often the poet is driven to a private printing in which he foots the bill, or part of the bill, for publication, in the hope that he will be recognized and later attract a commercial publisher. A few of the "vanity presses" are honestly concerned with the poet's welfare and give him his fair share of whatever sales take place. The rest are shady businesses which dupe and drain the naive young writer or the naive amateur writer of any age. Even the most altruistic and aesthetically alert commercial houses find it difficult to publish many books of verse, for most poetry falls in the "prestige" category of unprofitable but worthy books which are printed partly as a public service and partly to add tone to the seasonal list. As publishing costs rise, the break-even point (the sales figure which insures no loss to the publisher) also rises. Poetry offerings must be compensated for by large sales of other kinds of books if the publisher is to survive. While there is some hope that the paperbacks can make a go of poetry, especially in the form of anthologies, the plain fact is that costs always seem to prohibit both the printing of large amounts of poetry and the suitable rewarding of the poet.

The main drawback in poetry publishing is of course the very small sales volume. The cost of printing a book is not at all proportional to the number of copies sold; most of the expense lies in setting up plates, so that the decision to publish implies large costs. Poetry sells so poorly in the United States that one may say the poet has no market in any effective economic sense. His audience is simply too small to support his activities, the supply of serious verse far outstripping the demand. Poetry sales are both low and distinctly concentrated in a few big cities and college towns. It has been estimated that over eighty percent of all contemporary verse sold in book form is bought in four or five cities. Booksellers in smaller cities, especially outside the Northeast, do not stock much current poetry. One sign of this state of affairs is the regularity with which good books by good poets are remaindered, or sold some years after original publication at a ridiculous fraction of their announced price.

Sales of poetry to magazines are not much better. Serious modern poets rarely sell to any magazine of large circulation, since the editors tend to accept only slick verse or humorous fillers. The so-called "middlebrow" publications, such as *Harpers* and *The Atlantic Monthly,* print some excellent poetry but cannot afford to pay very high prices for it. *The New Yorker* and *The Saturday Review* are the real exceptions, for they publish modern poets regularly and have sufficient circulation to pay them well. The "little magazines" and critical reviews, some of which maintain scrupulous standards of quality, can make only a token payment or none. An interesting commentary on the tradition of non-payment appears in the prospectus for a new publication, *Poetry Broadside;* the editor, Barbara Romney, sets forth as an optimistic article of faith that "a poetry publication *can* exist which will be completely self-supporting and which will be able to pay its contributors for their work." The little magazines—exciting, earnest, and short-lived—perform an outstanding service to art by encouraging experiment and printing work by the young unknowns. But they cannot, by their very nature, help the poet much financially, despite the fact that one of the reasons for founding them is, according to Hoffman, Allen, and Ulrich, "a desire to overcome the commercial or material difficulties which are caused by the introduction of any writing whose commercial merits have not been proved." The situation seems fairly constant: it is worth recalling that one of Ezra Pound's most bitter attacks in his 1913 resumé of the poet's condition in America (*Patria Mia*) was directed at the magazine editors who refuse to consider any poetry which does not appear immediately palatable to a large audience.

In addition to direct compensation from the sale of poetry, there are certain indirect opportunities for the poet's economic maintenance. One of these is the possibility of winning one of the several prizes awarded for excellent work, such as the Pulitzer, Bollingen, or Nobel. Obviously, however, the prizes are few and generally go

147

to already well established poets. They cannot be counted on by an individual planning his year's expenses, although certainly they are most welcome when they come. While the rare prize may help support the recipient's next artistic venture, it is probably more important as a signal of the poet's distinction and an evidence that poetry as a career does not go totally unrecognized in this society. More significant than such chance windfalls are fellowships, livings, and gifts of various kinds; there are more of these, and they lend some stability to the economic aspects of the poet's immediate future. The artist knows where his next several meals are coming from, and although some few complain that this kind of support is debilitating—making the writer an over-secure and art-colonized pet—most are more than pleased with a respite from financial care. Perhaps the outstanding plums are invitations to live in art colonies, where one can be as isolated as he chooses and yet enjoy the frequent company of fellow poets, painters, and composers. For instance, at two of the prominent centers, Yaddo and McDowell, the poet has a pleasant climate, most expenses paid, and the room of his own that Virginia Woolf prescribed for sustained creative effort.

There are also a number of jobs which require rather light duties and are usually given to persons of some reputation. The host gains by having an artist around the house, and the artist gains a good deal of leisure. Poets often give much of themselves in such positions, teaching and guiding the young, and inspiring by the example of their personal devotion to craft. Guest residencies and temporary lectureships at various universities, as well as staff positions at certain of the summer writing conferences, fall in this category. Perhaps the symbolically most significant "living" on this order is the post of Consultant in Poetry to the Library of Congress. The Consultant, chosen on the basis of a major poetic reputation, is responsible for maintaining the Library's poetry services and increasing its excellent collection of recordings by contemporary poets. Although his fellow poets may often dispute the artistic merit of the occupant, and his direct functions may be centered around supplying uplifting quotations from nineteenth-century poets for legislators' purple flights, the position is nevertheless important as our single state-supported recognition of the poet's existence. The Consultant can make much or little of the job, but he is in an unusual spot to influence the intellectual life of Washington and to encourage young poets. He can also put poetry in the news, for better or worse, because the capital is saturated with journalists in search of copy. On the other hand, the Consultant's office is not precisely a tourist attraction and Library guards have been known to profess ignorance of office or poet.

Finally, one must mention the sheer windfalls which occasionally come the artist's way. Like prizes, these pleasant rewards are unpredictable and can scarcely be part of a rational economic outlook. Yet their rarity does

149

not negate the existence of a kind of informal patronage. Indeed, gifts from wealthy persons or non-repayable "loans" have been vital in the careers of several modern poets. For the obvious reason that dollars and cents are a more strictly tabooed topic than sex in this country, and that patrons tend to avoid the publicity that might clutter the garden with hungry writers, it is very difficult to learn the nature and extent of patronage today. A few commercial ventures might also be seen as windfalls. An amusing example was the experience of Conrad Aiken, who began hurriedly to throw away an "advertisement" in the morning mail when the figure of $750 caught his eye; this sum was offered him for a one-page poem to grace the annual publication of a pharmaceutical laboratory, a poem he readily contrived.

When all the possibilities are exhausted, however, it is still quite clear that most poets must earn a living by doing something else than poetry. What the "something else" should be is a question on which poets' opinions are divided. A large number feel that the responsibility of a regular occupation need not interfere with their poetry, and some maintain that their remunerative jobs actually contribute to the artistic task by affording varied experience and the refreshment of an alternative, contrasting métier. Among the latter are certain professional and business men. William Carlos Williams and Merrill Moore, both physicians, drew heavily on their medical lives when writing poetry; far from being internally split by their two vocations, they insisted that they

150

would be unhappy and perhaps less creative if writing were their sole activity. Richard Eberhart, in his years as a business executive, believed that business routine imposed a needed discipline and that evenings and holidays provided enough time for poetry. Perhaps the best-known instance of occupational doubling was the late Wallace Stevens, vice president of a large insurance company and highly respected modern poet.

The major issues seem to be how the content of the other job fits with poetry, and how it affects the availability of leisure. Most writers think the alternative job should not be too closely allied to poetry because the tasks might tend to blur and the creative energies might be adulterated. Yet people do not have unlimited ranges of talent, so very often the only position a poet can comfortably fill is literary or semi-literary, such as prose writing, editing, or criticism. Another job close to poetry is academic work; many poets are teachers of English, and despite the traditional horror of mixing pedagogy and creativity they appear to be happy and productive. Those who teach contend that it is a satisfactory complement to writing, while those who do not often see the university as a carefully designed trap in which artists are hamstrung if not prostituted. Teacher-poets report that many university appointments are better suited to the poet's needs today than has been true in the past, since some administrators have come to realize that writers require leisure and are not overloading them with class hours.

Poets are strongly opposed to jobs which are believed to consume talent and energy at a rapid pace. They cite such high-pressure occupations as newsmagazine writing or movie writing. These kinds of activity, it is felt, demand a wholesale allegiance which the artist cannot give. At the other extreme, there is a favorite conceit that the poet should earn his bread by manual labor, preferably in some pastoral pursuit. Few if any practicing poets of the first rank, however, are actually farmers or carpenters. The professions of law and medicine, and the business world, are realistically about as far from literary matters as the poet gets. Most writers have to double up on the one outstanding skill they possess—facility with language—and are thus employed in some region of the literary landscape, be it university or publishing house.

In general, poets testify that it makes no great difference what occupational path is followed: if a person is an artist he will manage in some way to continue his work. They do insist on freedom from pressure and a certain amount of leisure. The poet's acute awareness might be over-stimulated by a too demanding job and his vision might be narrowed by forced concentration on routine. The necessity of privacy for the poet's own labors, his required opportunity to isolate himself, implies that minimum leisure must be available. But at bottom the poetic talent and its habitual exercise rest on inner resources which are only indirectly affected by the specific form of earning a living.

Since patronage is rare and uncertain, and poetry does

not itself provide an adequate income, the question of subsidy naturally arises. The question is highly theoretical in this country, for poets fully expect to hold other jobs and the likelihood of organized subsidy is remote. Yet it raises interesting problems in the relation of the artist to his society. It is just to ask the poet to perform his creative job as a sideline? In the past, at many times and places, certain sinecures have been reserved for artists; they have sometimes been placed on the public payroll as valued representatives of the state. Racine's salary was steadily increased by the French monarchy, his job being to write plays, and the Renaissance princes supported artists in substantial numbers. Some modern American poets favor subsidy as the answer to the artist's economic disability. Ezra Pound, one of the staunchest proponents of subsidy, imagined the ideal arrangement to include a central academy where a hundred or more artists might work in perfect freedom from want. (Pound, however, like most poets, thought in terms of minimum survival rather than luxury; a revealing anecdote points out that he once returned half of a sum he had received from a patron, saying it was too much for a single year's subsistence and recommending that the other half go to a second poet.) In *Patria Mia* he prophesied for the nation:

> Yet this much is certain, if America has any
> desire to be a center of artistic activity she must
> learn her one lesson from the Ptolemies. Art was
> lifted into Alexandria by subsidy, and by no

153

other means will it be established in the United States.

In the same book Pound also has a memorable paragraph on the image of the starving artist who, according to legend, creates work of at least as high a quality as his better fed brothers:

> Villon is the stock example of those who advocate the starvation of artists, but the crux is here, to wit, that Villon had nothing whatsoever to gain by producing a bastard art. No harpies besought him for smooth optimism, for patriotic sentiment, and for poems "to suit the taste" of our readers. If he had nothing to lose by one sort of writing he had equally little to gain by any other.

Relatively few contemporaries endorse Pound's plea for outright subsidy. Some note that the ideal situation for the artist is a relation to a generous patron like Lorenzo de Medici. Others advance the notion that artists should be subsidized on a scale less than that of an adequate salary but great enough to close the gap between artistic earnings and a reasonable livelihood. Most poets, however, oppose subsidies for a variety of reasons: possible restrictions on creative freedom; encouragement of mediocrity; unnecessary character of such support when poets do in fact survive and continue to write.

It is impossible to describe the poet's economic situa-

154

tion with real accuracy because the contemporary scene shows so much diversity in career paths and so many combinations of potential sources of support. The paramount fact is the obvious one: poetry does not return its author a living wage, and hence he must adopt a second occupation unless he is born to wealth or marries a rich wife. At least one observer has remarked that women appear to be comparatively more numerous in contemporary American arts and letters than they have been in other countries or other historical eras. Perhaps an important reason for the large numbers of women artists is found in the economic facts of life: it is far easier for a woman to justify her existence without demonstrating a capacity for material success. A poet supported by her parents or her husband is not subject to the scorn which would greet a man in a comparable situation. When this economic leverage is combined with the social and psychological patterns which tend to bring the female and artist roles close together, it is apparent that the heavy representation of women in the ranks of highly regarded poets is not at all accidental. The poetic career in the United States, with its many financial and social hazards, is simply more comfortable for women than for men.

Economic renunciations are patently not the only obstacles to a career in poetry. Money and prestige tend to go hand in hand in our society, and the poet does not ordinarily command very much of either. Of course we do credit professors with some social standing, despite their low pay, and Supreme Court justices with high status despite their middling if comfortable salaries. But these figures perform chores which have an obvious utility. Even our outrageously overpaid entertainers, while they scarcely contribute to the world's work, undeniably have a vast audience which is presumed to enjoy their efforts. As Speier has so beautifully expressed the poet's station:

> Since the poet is not stirred by any desires to change this world, to make a world, as it were, he would irritate those who suffer and struggle, were it not for his pleasing art. Sufferings, injustice, agonies, the perishing gods of man, triumphant evil and sublimity in anguish—all this is thrown onto the playground of fate at which the poet looks without horror or disgust, and without indignation. Indeed, he pays no less attention to the stark and the evil than to the lovely and the sweet. He sees what is and never pales.

There seems little doubt, considering the mixed feeling with which the general American public regards poets (if indeed it regards them at all), that the poet decidedly irritates "those who suffer and struggle" and that his "pleasing art" is pleasing to only a very few. It is well that he is as unflinching as Speier perceives, for in addition to economic disability he suffers from acute lack of recognition and wide audience appeal. On whom then does he lean for the spiritual support, the reinforcement of morale that all men need?

The general public is seldom seen by modern poets as an important source of encouragement; the public does not read serious verse, or if reading it may often be relied on to misunderstand it. Many poets remark that letters of praise or interest from persons unknown to them tend to applaud the work for the wrong reasons—or to be written by the wrong persons. Contrary to one of the stereotypes of our times, the writer is not eager to be misunderstood; his pride is not enhanced by having someone admire the lovely sentiment of a poem whose intent is ironic or satirical. The unintended consequences of loosing a poem on the public need not be, but often are, harrowing to the conscientious professional. To be read by the wrong persons indicates that the artist is not having his desired effect, that his work may seem temporarily wasted because it is ignored by the kind of readers he respects. W. H. Auden gives a succinct analysis of this dilemma in *Poets at Work:*

> The ideal audience the poet imagines consists of the beautiful who go to bed with him, the powerful who invite him to dinner and tell him secrets of state, and his fellow-poets. The actual audience he gets consists of myopic schoolteachers, pimply young men who eat in cafeterias, and his fellow-poets. This means that, in fact, he writes for his fellow-poets.

Although some contemporaries confess to a desire for

157

mass popularity, public acclaim is on the whole too im-
probable to be a factor in the career. The poet says, "the
more readers the better," but insists that a big audience
is not important to his continuing artistic effort. There
is a certain fear that great popularity might be cause or
effect of diluted quality, that the only easily available
route to popular success involves a prostitution of verse.
This apprehension demonstrates yet another parallel
between today's artist and scientist, their common fear
that popularity and professional integrity may be basi
cally incompatible. Robert Frost once made an engaging
rejoinder which might indicate that if wide reputation
both critical and popular, has been achieved, the poet'
sureness of his own worth resolves this question. When
asked whether he wrote for the "little magazines," he
said to have replied, "No, I'd just as soon make love i
lover's lane." Most poets, however, are more concerne
that their readers be aesthetically select than that they l
numerous; they aver that the poet's contemporary aud
ence has probably never been very large and look to th
judgment of posterity rather than to immediate acclair
It seems inevitable that poets' indifference to broad rea
ership should have a defensive undertone, an element o
petulance in the face of public disregard. Some poe
have conceded that it is a "feigned indifference." Other
take the offensive by blasting the low level of publi
taste, and certainly both a withdrawn indifference and
defiant aggression are well recognized reactions to strain

If the general public does not shore up the poet'

morale, he must gain his rewards from more specialized publics. The primary characteristic of the specialized audience is of course literary sophistication. The writer's own family and friends, while they afford him comfort and delight in the daily round, are not directly inspiring in his role as poet unless they happen to possess literary taste and judgment. It simply does not matter to the poet, with a few notable exceptions, whether or not his wife or children like his latest creation; their applause may be warming, but their critical faculties and perspective may be untrustworthy. The situation is somewhat different with friends, partly because the artist's friends are apt to be literary and aesthetically perceptive, although one poet remarks that to depend on friends is to remain essentially an amateur. But there is usually an overlap here, and the fusion of critic and friend is an important source of the erratic and strained interpersonal relations often found in artists as a group. Again and again, poets state that if they could have five or six people who truly appreciate their work, they would not ask for more. There is recurrent emphasis on the "few true perceivers" who understand and critically sympathize with one's work, who are strict but yet rightly gauge the intrinsic discrepancy between a vision conceived and a poem executed.

Critical support is by far the most significant, inspiring new efforts and affording satisfaction with the completed work. Poets wait for the response of respected critics and take that response seriously. Critics are peers in the artis-

159

tic tradition of exclusive excellence, colleagues who are thought capable of discriminating assessment. While poets distinguish among critics, and are far from agreement on whose opinion is most consistently worthy, they generally affirm that critical response as a whole is their vital source of support. A few artists question the power and responsibility exercised by critics, but none is really immune to professional reaction. It is almost universally felt that critics are fellow-craftsmen, and in fact they often are other poets assuming the critic's role.

A natural result of the poet's dependence on such a small but powerful group as critics and his fellow writers is the tendency toward an artistic closed circle, the familiar spectacle of poets writing for critics and for one another, and vice versa. Although it is hard to see what other recourse the writer has in America today, poets especially and literate citizens generally are uneasy about the situation. We know our society is composed of specialists, and no one expects the chemist or physician or lawyer to write for a wide audience, yet we cannot escape the conviction that the poet is more than a technical expert and that his voice should resound more loudly than it does at present. The image of the artist spans Western society from its older, less specialized days, when many men were expected to do many things, to the modern era of narrowly distinctive function and competence. The artist whose poems do not emit the ring of common evaluative and stylistic coin comes to be thought deviant or cultist. Actually, the poet who has traditionally been

160

the "whole man" seems now to be in one sense an esoteric expert whose prospective audience has also become
split and specialized. The width of his potential appeal
is an unsolved question, and probably rests as much on
the scope of shared values and symbolic meanings in the
total culture as on the poet's own attempt to elaborate
the universal in the unique.

The picture of economic and spiritual support is not
then a bright one for the poet. Certainly his career is far
closer to Eliot's "mug's game" than to what we ordinarily
think of as a profession, such as law or medicine. Yet
modern poets do not tend to choose expatriation, to flee
the American circumstance for one more promising, as
did so many of their predecessors. Although many poets
point to England or France, Spain or Italy as a more
congenial artistic clime, they believe that a permanent
escape from their own country might be psychologically
impossible and artistically unwise or unnecessary. One
cannot really avoid his social roots by an attempt to
transplant them, and in any case America is "all right"
for poetry. Any place is "all right," since the artist's
inner integrity overcomes the rigors of neglect and discouragement.

The career is an inward thing, buttressed by the poet's
energy and self-confidence. In this unfolding of self, this
exaltation of consciousness, the individual-as-artist is
superior to the social climate in which he finds himself.
Considerations of income and prestige, audience and applause, are in the last analysis important but not basic:

161

they score the surface of the career, but are probably not determining influences on the lifelong development of the genuine poet. The poet is tough and has a seemingly boundless capacity for self-nourishment. He is drawn along by the game itself, by the strictly chosen imperative to fulfill the creative task. Allport's characterization of genius captures the undertone which makes the causal problems in the poetic career understandable:

> And there is the case of genius. A skill takes possession of the man. No primitive motivation is needed to account for his persistent, absorbed activity. It just *is* the alpha and omega of life to him.

Perhaps we are left, at the end, with the not too cryptic query, "Why do dancers dance?"

Views of the Self as Poet

CHAPTER VI

> Modern poets, in one sense, are the poets we
> know least about, and until time has made clear
> to us (and to them) their whole intent, until
> time has completed the circle whose arc they are
> now projecting, the poets themselves are likely
> to be their own best guides to themselves.
>
> —John Ciardi

> It is evident that a faith in their vocation,
> mystical in intensity, sustains poets.
>
> —Stephen Spender

A MAN'S IMAGE OF HIMSELF is always a critical feature
of his personality and a potent influence on his social
behavior. Poets' views of their activities, of their actual
and desired place in the universal scheme of things, are
among the most important influences shaping what will
in fact occur. Many years ago the sociologists Thomas
and Znaniecki advanced the axiom that, "If men define
situations as real they are real in their consequences";
this recognition of the power of subjective forces may be

paraphrased thus: If poets define poetry as real it is real in its consequences. They do so define it, and the consequences are immense.

Essentially, poets say, their proper role is to write poetry. The statement is not as absurdly obvious as it might appear, for it has several implications. The creative process, the individual grappling with language, is seen to lie at the heart of the poet's self-conception; he is not missionary, politician, or prophet but a craftsman engaged in writing as pure art. He stresses the work of art as an object, rather than the idiosyncracies of the artist's person, and he subsists on intense desire for artistic excellence. The poet's immersion in technical craft is furthered by his relative lack of concern with the tangible supports of a career or the gratifications of response from many readers. He does not write directly *for* an audience, although he hopes that an audience may overhear what he has written in self-exploration and self-clarification.

While poets are well aware of the long range social consequences of their work, they do not today commonly aim for any specific audience reaction other than aesthetic delight. They speak of their role not in terms of its consequences for others but in terms of the intrinsic rewards of creative devotion. Teaching and preaching inevitably occur, but they are seen as by-products of creative fascination and pleasure rather than ends to be deliberately pursued. The poet teaches himself, writes for himself, and in so doing provides vicarious experi-

164

ence for others. One might say that the first function of poetry is to clarify the writer's experience to himself, while the less obvious, implicit function is to clarify experience for others through the burning lens of a personal response to life.

Given this mode of self-definition, it is apparent that the tension which might be expected to prevail between the poet's realistic position and some more idealized version of his hoped-for existence is seldom tragically acute. Poets have to some extent made their peace with modern society by adopting a picture of themselves which is relatively impervious to the hazards of their circumstances. The poet is still the true revolutionary, but his tactics are more nearly those of an aesthetic fifth column or a small reconnaissance patrol than of massed battalions under a battle flag. It is of course question-able how much of the artist's insistence on privacy and self-sufficiency is a reasoned conclusion that this is the way things should be, and how much must be seen as a defensive reaction which rationalizes necessity into vir-tue. The poet can obviously make the best of a bad show by reiterating his indifference to neglect.

To Americans bred on dreams of showy public success, the poet's almost stoic acceptance of worldly rejection may seem incomprehensible or at best humiliating. The artist, however, while he has humility in the face of artistic mastery, does not give the impression of a hum-ble man. He is not self-deprecating; if he has not the Shavian effrontery to compare his work favorably to

Shakespeare's, he nevertheless takes a deep and confident pride in the role of poet. He is resilient without callousness and bold without bravado. Modern poets do not seem worried that they are such resoundingly "unacknowledged legislators of mankind." They view themselves as judicial rather than legislative, and are content if their judgments have an implicit relevance for society. In his own eyes the poet is neither culture hero nor commissar of aesthetic enlightenment, but a responsible citizen doing a responsible job.

If the core of the poet's conception of his proper activities is the writing itself, it is just as surely true that this writing has implications for society at large. How does the modern poet believe his work affects the civilization in which he lives? In answer to such a question, the poet typically considers poetry as an artistic fact rather than himself as individual voice; he lives in his work while writing it, and if his personal chord is to outlast his own mortality the work must endure. Taking all time as his stage, he contends that his influence on future generations may be at least as great as—and usually greater than—his effect on his own era. The idea of the poet as prophet, so pronounced in mythology and antique religion, finds contemporary expression in the belief that the poet is in some way ahead of his time.

Today, of course, he is no longer credited with foretelling specific events but rather with enunciating novel perceptions and values which may foreshadow changed ways of seeing in the larger society. Many poets think of the artist as part of a phalanx which forges ahead, lighting the way for the generality of men who are less gifted perceivers. This theme is emphasized, for instance, in Conrad Aiken's philosophy of art. To Aiken, the poet summarizes contemporary experience and relates it to past and future times. But since the public does not have the poet's heightened awareness, he seems to be in advance, and his keenest insights become significant only to later generations. He is thus the only true contemporary, speaking *for* but not *to* his own time.

The poet as hostage to the future, unransomed and unread by his fellows, again becomes a protective image for those who suffer present neglect. If one's role is not now exalted, its fruits may nevertheless merit the acclaim of audiences yet to come. Yet the poet's banking on posterity must be seen as more than a fantasy, more than a salve for quotidian injury. Artistic history supports the argument that men often do win a delayed recognition, that the artist's status in his own society is not necessarily a valid measure of his reputation or intrinsic worth in the long run. The modern poet has excellent precedent for writing verse which is, as Herbert Read succinctly expresses it, "poetry inspired by the expectation of a 'paper eternity.' "

Another aspect of the poet's subjective vision is his designation as a representative "stater of experience." He speaks for other men, and by increasing his own awareness he also enhances the general level of awareness. In his role as public voice or conscience he sharpens

167

our perception and seasons our wisdom, but always by example rather than overt admonition. Poets also stress the obvious fact that their close involvement with language, a social vehicle, implies the working out of a truly social role at the very instant when they appear to the casual eye to be isolated and unique.

The poet then believes his role to be central in society whether or not society is at any given moment prepared to recognize it as central. He is able to accommodate, and to some extent resolve, the tension between the artist's contemporary neglect and his self-portrait as a potentially great achiever. Poetry in the perspective of centuries, and the modern poet in his quiet confidence, attest that the reconciliation of these widely divergent notions of the poet's role rests more heavily on faith and historical sensitivity than on a wishful self-delusion.

If he sees himself as important, an importance of integrity rather than grandeur, how does he respond to the shabby treatment accorded him on the American scene? Surprisingly enough, the poet does not think matters are "as bad as all that"; while his remarks may often be tinged with hostility and bitterness, he is disinclined to whimper. Many poets feel the American environment has been comparatively good to them, that the public definition of their role neglects but does not crush. Naturally they would prefer to be more highly regarded, but the poetic task as they view it is so impregnably worth-while that they see little use in crying over spilt stanzas. There is congenial acceptance of the situation, an acceptance nearly always matched by a certain grim resolution. The artist in America has to be tough, but the toughness is perhaps best described as an unobtrusive inner resiliency. Quiet firmness is more characteristic than violent protest. Life to the poet, after all, is as often to be hugely enjoyed as to be grimly endured. He is not a vulnerable Kafka hero groping in a nightmare world but a highly competent and clear-headed member of society. The poet is playful, endowed with extra measures of delight and irony, and he openly confesses that it is fun to do what he does.

But in return for his society's disregard, he demands freedom to go his own way. If he has to live a difficult life, marginal to the main concerns of most fellow-citizens, then he wants it understood that he cannot be expected to excite himself about every swerve and shallow in the course of public attention. The poet knows things that need doing, and his first priority is to write verse rather than to serve on committees or respond to the instant dicta of majority opinion. Archibald Mac-Leish counters the demand that the poet be a political or social loyalist and at the same time makes an important statement about his inevitable solitude:

Does Madame recall our responsibilities? We are
Whores Fraulein: poets Fraulein are persons of
Known vocation following troops: they must sleep
    with
Stragglers from either prince and of both views:

169

The rules permit them to further the business of
    neither.

The things of the poet are done to a man alone
As the things of love are done—or of death when
    he hears the
Step withdraw on the stair and the clock tick only

Neither his class nor his kind nor his trade may
    come near him
There where he lies on his left arm and will die:
Nor his class nor his kind nor his trade when the
    blood is jeering
And his knee's in the soft of the bed where his love
    lies:

I remind you Barinya the life of a poet is hard—
A hardy life with a boot as quick as a fiver:
Is it just to demand of us also to bear arms?

When the poet gauges himself, measures his life and
work against some standard of accomplishment, he naturally refers to other writers of the past and present. One
reason for the seeming inconsistency with which he takes
his art seriously while resigning himself to the bits and
crumbs of social reward is that he does not compare the
poet's role with the businessman's or politician's or
scientist's. To make such a comparison would not only
aggravate his deprivations of money and prestige but
would be basically irrelevant. Business and professional
élites, while sharing certain functions of leadership and

170

intelligence with the artist, are differently recruited and trained and are essentially different in the means and goals of their tasks. The poet wisely refers himself instead to the company of modern poets and to selected figures in the artistic tradition.

In the United States the poet can ordinarily feel himself to be an equal of his contemporaries. They are "all in it together"; scarcely anyone can make a living from poetry and very few gain noticeable public recognition. The sense of artistic fraternity does not, however, shield the poet from the rigors of invidious comparison. Rather, it moves the competition to another level than the usual one of wealth and privilege, to the stage of *aesthetic* judgments. Many vocations other than poetry, it is true, are marked by comparison and reward on intrinsic technical grounds—scholarship, science, medicine, cabinet-making, and so on; but modern poetry is unique in that vocational superiority is not necessarily accompanied by tangible evidence of success. The strains of aesthetic inequality, as seen for instance in changes the self-portrait may undergo with the rise and fall of critical favor, are very real. Yet they too are cushioned not only by the sense of fellowship in art but by the poet's special historical consciousness. His chief reference group, or basis of comparison, in addition to his contemporaries, is made up of the great voices of the past.

By placing himself in historical perspective, the poet is able to mitigate feelings of inferiority and disappointment whether they arise from lack of critical esteem or

171

lack of popular success. Critical fashion varies, and what
Malcolm Cowley terms the "literary stockmarket" shows
that wide fluctuations in reputation occur from century
to century and even from decade to decade. Future recognition is a distinct possibility, and it is a very comforting hypothesis to entertain since it cannot be tested
within the writer's own lifetime. Looking back, the poet
sees many whose "failure" has been transformed by
changes of taste into remarkable achievement. With
respect to external circumstance, again, it is established
that the true artist's work has survived regardless of the
ease or hardship he experienced during his lifetime. If
the modern notes that Shakespeare or Tennyson or
Browning enjoyed greater respect and affluence than the
poet now can muster, he also recalls the tribulations of
Villon or Rimbaud or Melville. The indignities of one's
personal artistic or material position are also finally
softened by the philosophy of a "republic of letters" in
which each individual contributes his peculiar talent.
Thus the often satirized distinction between major and
minor poets expresses the idea that an artist's work may
be valuable and excellent without having great bulk or
special originality of style. Art parallels science in its
embracing nature as a company of equals who welcome
any increment, however small, to the total fund.

The insulation poets receive from their small craft
group and their keen apprehension of past and future
time cannot, of course, absorb all the shocks implicit in
a marginal social position. Drastic conflicts between the

172

poet's values and the values of American mass society, lack of support, and the rude neglect or hostility with which the public views his role must stimulate some anxiety and resentment. In rueful or cynical fashion the writer can recount stories of indifference, insult, misunderstanding, and perhaps worst of all, heavy-handed "tolerance." He meets many persons, not patrons, who adopt a patronizing attitude. He is often reminded of the fact that he is not *"really* working" and questioned with, "What do you *do* all the time?" Examples of the poet's accidents in the mundane world are legion. One writer tells of his pride on being complimented by a lady visitor about the fine condition of his garden, only to have her spice the balm by remarking that, after all, since he was a poet he had nothing else to do but tend his plants. Another poet offers the tale, which one can only pray is apocryphal, of a dinner party to which he and his wife, also a poet, were invited by a noted dowager. Seated near their hostess, they heard her loudly instruct the maid: "Don't serve the John Does any soup or appetizer; they're poets, you know, and not used to having very much to eat. It might harm them."

An interesting sidelight on the poet's role, and on his defense of his chosen calling, may be obtained by assessing his attitude toward science. Scientific thought and practice have often been seen as the great competitor with the arts for the allegiance of the modern world, and the scientist's popular prestige has risen as the artist's has fallen into neglect or confusion. The poet's view of science and art may be conveniently focused on the question of a psychological or sociological approach to the artist and his work. Is such research likely to be valuable or harmful? Can it add to what we already know about poetry?

Poets' answers to these questions emphasize again their feelings of independence and of a certain inviolableness about the artistic task. They are not in the main hostile to scientific inquiry but rather indifferent to its direct effect on their own craft. This is not, of course, to say that poets do not recognize the power of science in shaping everyone's view of the world, or that they deny the general influence of scientific developments on their own behavior. It is merely that, while acknowledging the rightful place of science, the poet does not believe scientific method really competes with his own or encroaches on his creative province. Many artists feel the scientific approach to art to be unrewarding, but few term it bad or dangerous. The poet says to the psychologist, "You *can't* hurt me," and proceeds to explain that science cannot probe the meaning of a poem or the writer's creative endeavor. Science never has the "last word" on artistic matters; it does not succeed in going beyond the artistic formulation, but only in attacking phenomena from a different angle. Thus one poet comments that a specific poetic image *is* the last analysis, and no matter how many relations, extensions, and explanations of the image the scientist may offer, he never goes *deeper than* the original figure of poetic speech. If many poets tick off scientific research into their field, however, it should be noted that some generously welcome any investigation. On the premise that something new may be discovered, the poet who is hospitable to science contends that any addition to the store of human knowledge and consciousness is to the good since it enlarges the perceptual range of the artist.

The poet is autonomous and insists that he can and should continue working his time-honored artistic vein. His belief in the integrity and vitality of his art outweighs all discouragement. He is not cowed by neglect, or by the superior prestige of science, or by anything else. The crucial element in his own view of self is that "faith in vocation, mystical in intensity" to which Spender testifies. Poetic tradition is exceedingly durable; when the poet defines his role as important he does not brashly claim a place in the sun as an isolated individual, but envisions himself as a link, however great or small, in a chain reaching back to Homer and the ancient Chinese lyricists. Modern poets know the craft they have embraced is honorable and enduring. They keep the vocational faith and find both solace and inspiration in the achievements of the past. Their activity is rooted in a symbolic and temporal largeness of view which places the poet's current "loss" of function and lack of recompense in proper perspective. The poet is not a lonely marginal man but a member of a vast company forged by common devotion. As Lionel Trilling observes in his brilliant essay on Scott Fitzgerald, our estimate of a man begins with his estimate of himself. Like Fitzgerald, who could seriously compare himself to the master novelists, modern poets think in terms of the artistic heritage. In the blinding light of this heritage, their views of self are not grandiose but calmly realistic.

Poet To Poet

CHAPTER VII

> I make a pact with you, Walt Whitman—
> I have detested you long enough.
> I come to you as a grown child
> Who has had a pig-headed father;
> I am old enough now to make friends.
> It was you that broke the new wood,
> Now is a time for carving.
> We have one sap and one root—
> Let there be commerce between us.
> —Ezra Pound, "A Pact"

THE MODERN POET, even when he appears most isolated, is in one sense a member of a fraternal corps. While following his unique verbal destiny he yet belongs to a company of writers who share the common concerns of the poetic task, broadly conceived, however much they may differ in personal outlook or favored style. This feeling of shared identity and artistic fellowship anchors the poet who, in contemporary American life, may otherwise have scant experience of belonging.

In speaking of poets as "a group," it is important to

realize that the group is not the tightly knit, organized system of face-to-face relations which the term often calls to mind. The professional comradeship of poets is based on less tangible factors than weekly meetings or ceremonial rituals. Most communication among writers occurs at one remove, in the form of letters, reviews, literary gossip, and—by far the most significant and revealing—the created work itself. The special mark of the artist is of course precisely this, that one can know him very well indeed without ever having met him. Modern poets have a deep knowledge of one another and they are unified through their calling. Group bonds are implicit but real; one is justified in portraying an artistic community which underlies and modifies the poet's fierce independence.

The poetic fraternity does not display a firm structure of accepted relationships, a pronounced leader, or an obvious program of action. With the exception of small and, in the United States, temporary clusters of individuals who gather for a specific interest such as magazine editing or writers' conferences, poets do not usually speak of themselves as group members. Rather, one discerns an implied consensus on the central importance of the poet's calling and an unobtrusive but zealous faith in vocational destiny. These commonly held articles of agreement are supplemented by the unsystematic yet pervasive patterns of acquaintance, friendship, visiting, and hearsay. It is thus perhaps appropriate to think of modern American poets as a kind of extended family,

178

scattered in space and characterized by both the closeness of interest and the violence of dispute which often
mark familial life.

When a poet allies himself with a specific group, a
consciously cooperative body of fellow artists, his membership is likely to be both enthusiastic and brief. Such
a sub-group of the total artistic population obviously
can stress only a fragment of contemporary poetic interest
or a specialized regional emphasis. It may set the pace
for a limited time, particularly if its unifying force is a
genuine innovation in style or theme. Although coteries
have been numerous in the United States, they have
seldom attained great or lasting influence. Today the
select band of devotees is seldom held out as the total
context for the poet; most modern writers tend to emphasize the differences rather than the similarities between themselves and their peers. Perhaps because his
countrymen are, the American poet decidedly is not a
"joiner." He tries, in fact, to dissociate himself from any
hint of uniform doctrine. For instance, when the New
Criticism came under fire some years ago for its allegedly
totalitarian taint, several poets and critics who had been
identified with it announced vehemently that the New
Critics were exceedingly various in political and aesthetic
allegiance. Another example of the diverse tenets and
fleeting memberships which characterize the artistic sub-
group is seen in the history of the Fugitive poets, an
energetic and talented society which flourished at Van-
derbilt University in the 1920's. Their commitment

179

appears essentially to have been focused on the importance of a lively and experimental art rather than on any defined brand of work, and their subsequent careers have been notable for variety as well as distinction.

This country has known far less of the cult than have many others. In part the lack of unity among artists may be traced to general social and geographical conditions. We have not the cafés of Paris or the intimate physical compass of Britain. When an artistic haven such as Greenwich Village does develop, it tends to lose its savor and its appeal for the serious artist within a generation or two. If a vast continent and large population promote disunity and purely regional groupings, it can also be maintained that American society has been so inhospitable to the artist that self-confident coteries could not flourish. Whatever reasoning one may apply to the relative absence of collective action by American poets, however, the important feature today is the individual poet's determination to keep his group ties loose and to avoid any neat aesthetic label.

But the general picture of individualism and ideological uniqueness cannot, of course, stand alone. Well formed groups do arise from time to time, and their positive implications are many. They provide encouragement, inspire a sense of purpose, and, most significantly, afford a sympathetic if small audience. The desirability of an informed, responsive set of listeners or readers does not typically lead to the formation of a group; the Fugitives, however, were an excellent example of the stimula-

180

tion which may ensue if a group does arise, and more recently a number of poets in and around Boston have formed the habit of reading together at regular intervals. Participants in both the Fugitive and Cambridge circles report a feeling of gain from the collective process. The members constitute an effective sounding board, a source of alert criticism, and a locus of immediate responsive reward which the solitary artist must otherwise often forego.

A broader function of the small group becomes clear if we think of its influence on poetry as a whole rather than on individual members. The zealous band livens the poetic scene, generating excitement and ideas which are often sprightly if seldom new. Some public attention may be attracted by group readings or the inevitable manifestoes of artistic discontent. If a little magazine results from group deliberations, as is often the case, then poetry usually benefits on balance from the stirring up of the atmosphere and the publication of young writers who require print as balm and goad. The other side of the coin, and probably one basis of the suspicion with which contemporary poets regard the tight artistic group, is that a unifying aesthetic creed may at length draw the bonds too closely around individual members. Instead of stimulating poetry in general, the group life may come to impose unwelcome restrictions on those involved and to discourage any experiment following the first one; as the group ages, that is, it may come to adopt Calvin Coolidge's view that "we have had our revolution." Premature crystallization of form or theme may stunt the propensity for artistic variation and force adherence to doctrines which have lost their vigor.

A special instance of poetic grouping is the formation of committees or prize councils for some specific, limited task. These bodies are significant because they demonstrate both the willingness of poets to draw together for a common concern and their eagerness to disband when the purpose has been accomplished. Even committees which must function on an annual basis often adopt rotating membership as a protection against artistic monopoly or the growth of a rigid coterie. The patent functions of these gatherings may be described as very diverse: to award a prize, to assist a fellow-poet in distress, to make recommendations about policy for some source of patronage. Underlying the manifest ends, however, is the implicit purpose of expressing craft solidarity. The company of equals meets to reiterate a sense of artistic fellowship and professional exclusiveness; although its members differ in taste and talent they are unified by a belief in the significance of their art. Here too is a parallel with other professions such as law, medicine, or scholarship, in which intense rivalry within the broad professional group may be temporarily submerged for some mutually accepted and professionally representative purpose. It should also be noted that the dinner or tea, the committee meeting or literary cocktail party, serves as a vehicle for communicating gossip and news; the poet's isolation, his rejection of cramping group ties, is thus alleviated.

If, apart from these temporary clusterings, American poets may be seen as a large informal group or craft union, on whom do the poets depend for leadership? Artistic leadership is obviously a very special type of authority-by-example; since poets are not organized for specific goals or bound to any fixed program of action, they need not turn to authority in any consistent fashion. Dominance is subtle, and is often acknowledged only through stylistic imitation (which may or may not be deliberate) or an attitude of respect for the leader's critical judgments. Poets are usually loath to admit that another poet, especially if he is a contemporary still living, is truly a pace setter. Analysis of leadership in other settings, in the business and professional worlds, does however yield one dictum that seems particularly relevant to poetic leadership: the leader must be himself an expert at the common task. For instance, two of the figures to whom modern poets have long paid homage, T. S. Eliot and Ezra Pound, are master poets as well as critical arbiters.

The scarcity of channels for directly exercising power does not inhibit the growth of awesome power symbols. Delmore Schwartz can, for example, entitle an essay, "The Literary Dictatorship of T. S. Eliot." Leaders may, in general, be identified by the number and quality of references to them in dedications and critical essays. But lines of influence are not always explicit; all poets borrow from what has gone before, and a writer may be sincerely ignorant of the effect another writer has had upon him. Artistic leadership is in one respect similar

183

to artistic reputation itself, in that for contemporaries the jury is still out, and a person now viewed as a very important innovator or critic may bulk much less large from the perspective of another century than do some of his quieter fellows.

Leaders often initiate significant artistic activity by selecting younger poets for attention and encouragement. They are conversely chosen, and reinforced in their dominant positions, by being asked for advice and opinion. An interesting aspect of leadership is revealed in the operations of the little magazine. The small review, on its inception, usually looks to prominent poets for semi-official blessing or a "name" contribution. Its editor then prints, with great pride, a poem or a paragraph of encouragement from a major figure which constitutes a sort of benediction or artistic laying on of hands. The smile of enthusiasm, or the nod of knowingly shared irony, is particularly important to the young in poetry because the leader's assent provides recognition and approval in the absence of more formal criteria of just achievement.

It has sometimes been observed in studies of polity that the best man is not necessarily the best citizen. Civic responsibility, like personal agreeableness, is seldom exactly commensurate with an individual's talent for his vocation. Poets are able to make discriminating estimates of one another, according to whether they are gauging social utility, congeniality, or artistic merit. As with leaders, so with the generality of his peers, the poet

184

distinguishes talent from likeableness. Thus a good poet may be deprecated as a person even while his poems are most admired. One contemporary writer expresses the distinction by remarking that, "Most of the people one knows aren't poets, and most of the poets one knows aren't people."

Despite this aphoristic venom, however, modern poets seem to like one another quite as well as do members of any other craft. The jealousies and entanglements that make artistic friendships stormy matters are really what one might expect to find in an extended family or a professional élite. Poets care so very much for poetry, and invest so much of themselves in their work, that minor disagreements and personal slights are occasionally magnified into bitter campaigns. Sensitive creatures, plagued by sharp consciousness of the lineaments of their own and others' characters, may deal violent insult in situations where more prosaic men content themselves with mild reproof. Then too, as Miriam Gallaher has remarked, "The poet is highly articulate. Some good, going feuds among lesser souls just can't get beyond a pedestrian splutter; to a poet, shaping a good insult can seem a work of art." Many of the seeming unkindnesses and angers in the relation of poet to poet may also be traced to a professional code of candor; the poet does not pussyfoot or aim for silken public relations. He does not much care to be a "well-adjusted" cog in any social machine and his glad hand is reserved for joy rather than palmed off in the interest of a contrived harmony. The art of poetry is too important to be laden with hypocrisy and cant; it is hard enough to say what one means about another's poem or person without trying to say what one does not mean. And beneath the tensions, like a strong net, lie the deep, enduring friendships, the tender closeness of artistic fellowship. By reason of common sensitivity and knowledge, poets of all men can go "proudly friended."

The poet's relations to his fellow poets are obviously most significant to the study of poetry as a social activity, and this is the more true today when he has so little contact with a responsive general audience. Yet it is perhaps appropriate to mention a few further aspects of his relation to the anonymous or lay public, and to his immediate family. These other, non-professional relations actually reiterate and develop certain of the themes remarked both in professional group contexts and in the creative poetic process.

Those with whom the artist lives his daily life, his family and intimate friends, may be exposed to a very wide range of behavior. There are poets who act conscientiously as heads of families, "good providers," and devoted husbands and fathers. Others are much less stable in these respects; they find it difficult to maintain an enduring set of relationships, and their erratic movements partially confirm the Bohemian stereotype of poetic irresponsibility. The serious question to ask is, "Irresponsible to what or to whom?" The major factor in the often avowed notion that the poet is a bear to

186

live with seems to be his extraordinary devotion to his art. Like the physicist married to his laboratory, an artist may be so wedded to his art that other considerations become distressingly secondary. Many poets say that the artist is likely to be a poor risk for marriage, that he is inherently unstable in his human relations. They argue that this situation is inseparable from the calling, that a poet must be a poet first and an agreeable human being second. Many writers seem to require kid glove handling by the people close to them; in this vein the ideal poet's wife would be acutely sensitive to nuances in his personality and would brew a judicious tonic of deference and applause, domestic piety and heroic selflessness. The poet needs intense emotional support, but paradoxically he also needs a certain distance from others to preserve his psychological and vocational autonomy.

Poetic chronology rarely corresponds to Greenwich time, so the poet may be a breaker of engagements and a forgetter of appointments. The poem must sometimes take precedence over the dinner party; as Dudley Fitts once remarked, a poem is not something one can put off until next week. The sketch should not be overdrawn, since many writers live exceedingly well regulated lives in which a variety of tasks are nicely apportioned. Consider, for instance, the busy poet-physicians, Merrill Moore and William Carlos Williams, who squeeze an amazing bundle of activities into the daily round yet weave poetry into the very fabric of their lives. The im-

187

portant point is that when "selfishness" or waspish antics or familial tension are prominent, these less agreeable aspects of artistic existence should be related to the poet's vocational commitment. A startling absorption in the self when one is striving to create out of his own vitals is not the selfishness of an egoistic boor. Nor is the delicately tense posture of an explorer on the frontier of consciousness at all the same as the flighty course of a neurotically under-employed housewife.

The poet's optimal amount and intensity of social intercourse is an unsolved question, as it probably must be for all individuals who work persistently at a creative job. His contact with friends, students, admirers, and any other who come to his door tends to fluctuate widely through time. Many poets insist on the artist's need for frequent interaction with a variety of persons. They pursue what might be described as an individual cycle of "challenge and response," in which the writer goes out into the social world, retreats to create, then goes again to society for stimulation and verification. Richard Wilbur has spoken of the necessity for enlarging and testing the poet's inner world by a recurrent infusion from the outer world of events. In his autobiography, Stephen Spender analyzes the pattern of withdrawal and involvement as it affected him:

> Meeting people, receiving a large number of letters and invitations, and feeling under an obligation to reply to them, these are perhaps greater dangers to the writer than debauchery.

188

Social life is all the more dangerous because it is to some extent necessary to him. It is one of his main doors of entrance into the life of other people. . . . He is not protected by having an office and office hours. Unless he fights hard against them he is constantly exposed to interruptions.

I did not want to wear a mask, to exert my will, to choose among people, to judge before I knew them, whom I should see and whom not see; I felt that any such attitude would inevitably result in a kind of hardness from which my work would suffer, and which would be a far more serious sacrifice than the loss of time.

Many threads of poetic ideology and many facets of the poet's career in modern American society may be interestingly revealed in the case history of one poet. A single man's career, in and out of art, illustrates some of the problems contemporary writers face. Because this particular man, Ezra Pound, was projected into a public and controversial figure, his artistic and social role became a focus of attention. His personality and politics, his poetry and singular activities, stirred a renewed concern for the poet's role among artists, officials, and the general public.

189

The Affairs of Ezra Pound

CHAPTER VIII

The Rest

O helpless few in my country,
O remnant enslaved!

Artists broken against her,
A-stray, lost in the villages,
Mistrusted, spoken-against,

Lovers of beauty, starved,
Thwarted with systems,
Helpless against the control;

You who cannot wear yourselves out
By persisting to successes,
You who can only speak,
Who can not steel yourselves into reiteration;

You of the finer sense,
Broken against false knowledge,
You who can know at first hand,
Hated, shut in, mistrusted:

Take thought:
I have weathered the storm,
I have beaten out my exile.

Salvationists

I.

Come, my songs, let us speak of perfection—
We shall get ourselves rather disliked.
                                    —Ezra Pound

EZRA POUND is not a "typical" modern American poet.
His genius and his pathology, his artistic leadership and
his singular ideological tenets, mark him off as a distinct and unique figure. If Pound's is not a usual poetic
career, however, it is in some ways a representative and
enlightening one because of its very extremities. Pound's
style of personality, and his thrust toward an artistic destiny unencumbered by the demands of citizenship or
social convention, raised major issues of the artist's existence to the surface of public and critical consciousness. His arrest for treason following World War II, his
hospitalization as a mental patient, and his subsequent
receipt of the Bollingen Prize for excellence in poetry,
converged to stir up the reactions of his fellow poets
and a re-examination of the artist's right relation to
society.

Born in Idaho in 1885, Pound migrated to the East at
the age of fifteen. After studying at the University of

Pennsylvania and Hamilton College, he taught for short periods at both Pennsylvania and Wabash. A poet and a student of literature, he was apparently a spirited, controversial figure from the very first. As early as 1909, he was involved in fiery discussion and mutual criticism with William Carlos Williams. The two young poets were to follow vividly contrasting careers, although both maintained a lifelong devotion to poetry. Pound was to become the most alienated of expatriates, damning American life and art with equal vigor. He was noted for his Bohemian style of life, his passion, his irascible temperament; dismissed from the Wabash faculty on various charges, he later claimed that the only proved count was his fondness for a "Latin Quarter" mode of existence. Williams, on the other hand, heartily embraced a more or less conventional American heritage; in moderate, "normal" fashion he became a professional man and practiced medicine in a small New Jersey town. He renounced the garret and the expatriate's voyage for a comfortable middle-class home and a pattern of unequivocal service to his community.

Ezra Pound went to Europe after his brief experience in the academic world, taking with him a curious blend of violent disgust with his native country and earnest hope that it might one day flower as a haven of the arts. He never became wholly disengaged from the American scene, for he kept in close touch with poets and other friends while using this country as a hard wall to push against, a target for both diatribes and more optimistic exhortations. He lived for many years in England and France, writing much of the poetry and criticism which were to make him famous and establish him as a poet of the first rank. Pound joined remarkable lyric gifts with a wide if often sketchy knowledge of many literatures. In addition to his original poetry, he performed amazing translations from Chinese and other tongues. As a dedicated, entirely devoted artist, Pound fought to raise and refine critical standards. He was energetic in the welter of experimental movements which characterized the second and third decades of the century's poetry. He was now well on the way to the reputation Williams later pronounced:

> "Ezra Pound is one of the most competent poets in our language, possessed of the most acute ear for metrical sequences to the point of genius, that we have ever known."[1]

He rejected American values in many things, and was notably shocked at the condition of poetry:

> "I may be myopic, but during my last tortured visit to America I found no writer and but one reviewer who had any worthy conception of poetry, The Art."[2]

Pound also felt keenly the lack of support for the vocation and the obstacles to publication. In his first

---

[1] Norman, Charles: *The Case of Ezra Pound* (New York: The Bodley Press, 1948), p. 49.

[2] *Ibid.,* p. 25.

193

dealings with Harriet Monroe and *Poetry* magazine he noted that:

> "There is no other magazine in America
> which is not an insult to the serious artist and
> to the dignity of the art."[1]

His great dissatisfactions with the United States, as well as his reforming and teaching bent, are perhaps best revealed in the book he wrote in 1913, *Patria Mia.* Here he explores the bases of disenchantment and shrewdly analyzes American art at that time.

It has often been said of Pound that his influence would be immense even if his own poetry were negligible. While one may doubt that his critical canons would have won such wide acceptance were he not himself a poet of the first order, it is quite true that he exerted a profound force on other poets and on the flourishing development of the art through his enthusiastic guidance and his insistence on an austere excellence. As a leader of poets, he helped younger writers, flaying and coaxing them into their best work. As a polemicist and one who cared deeply about what happened to poetry, he was potent in keeping the craft alive and lively. His "discoveries" were numerous, and he had a talent for dealing with editors. Pound secured publication for many of his contemporaries and juniors; a roll call of those he pushed sounds like a comprehensive roster of the great modern poets:

---

[1] *Ibid.,* p. 24.

"Throughout his long and controversial career, Ezra Pound discovered or ballyhooed the
work of men who have since become renowned,
some of them crowned with the Nobel Prize for
Literature, such as the Irish poet, William But-
ler Yeats, and the Bengal poet, Rabindranath
Tagore. And he brought to the budding poetry
renaissance in the United States the impact and
inspiration of his technique and ideas."[1]

Pound's importance as a leader is well-illustrated by
his role in assisting the then newly-established *Poetry,*
which has since become perhaps the most influential,
and certainly the most venerable, of the little magazines.
He encouraged the publication from the start, sending
his own work and, as foreign correspondent, the best
poems of his contemporaries in England, France, and
other countries. A large number of American poets got
their start in *Poetry,* and to a considerable extent *Poetry*
got its start from Ezra Pound. His critical zeal was vital.
Harriet Monroe, the then editor, recalls:

"I could go on for many pages with Pound's
early letters. They were a tonic and an inspiration, for at that time, as I firmly believe, he was
the best critic living, at least in our specialty,
and his acid touch on weak spots was as fear-
somely enlightening as a clinic."[2]

---

[1] Norman, Charles, *op. cit.,* p. 23.
[2] Norman, Charles, *op. cit.,* p. 29.

195

Pound's leadership was of course not limited to American writers. His catholic interest and long European exile made him an international figure. With the writer and painter Wyndham Lewis, he was both prominent and provocative on the English literary scene. The little magazine *Blast,* an iconoclastic journal marked by his artistic intensity and his desire to reform those modern values he abhorred, was one index of this activity. Pound lived his campaigns with a high seriousness; note the earnestness with which he speaks, nearly thirty years later, of *Blast*:

> "And that manifesto was the best we could
> do then toward asserting what has now become
> known to the world, or at least to the European
> continent, as the crisis of the system."[1]

But Pound was also distinguished for qualities other than artistic leadership: egotism, arrogance, bitterness toward those who disagreed with him, devotion to idiosyncratic and crankish theories of economics and politics. William Carlos Williams recalls a startling example of his pride and prejudice:

> "But he always felt himself superior to anyone
> about him and could never brook a rival . . .
> He just lived on a different plane from anyone
> else in the world, a higher plane! . . . I remem-

---

[1] Rudge, Olga: "If This Be Treason—" (Tip. Nuova; Siena, Italy: 1948).

ber one April morning in 1909 we were passing
a church in Kensington, . . . We moved on, he
insisting upon being one step in advance of me
as always. I remember my brother once in the
same situation turned and walked off in the
opposite direction."[1]

His bitterness was well-known. Conrad Aiken failed
to attend a dinner party given in 1914 to launch *Blast,*
and over twenty years later Pound was still attacking
Aiken for neglecting his imperious summons.

All in all, Ezra Pound's poetic talent through the years
has outbalanced his flair for personal antagonism. As
professional poet, if not as entire human being, he has
commanded the homage of his fellow artists. His career
exemplifies several elements which any discussion of the
modern poet's social role must apprehend. Pound's dramatic alienation from certain critical values of Western
society, especially those of middle-class convention and
the commercial market, may be seen as an exaggeration
of a very common theme in artistic ideology. His history
further demonstrates the interplay of personal tensions
within the artistic fraternity, the significance of the little
magazine in poetic style and the poet's support, and the
special shape of artistic leadership. Finally and most importantly, Pound symbolizes the supreme vocational
faith and confidence in self which distinguish the poet

---

[1] Norman, Charles: *op. cit.,* p. 51.

who is committed to a life in art. While Pound's cantankerous and overweening self-glorification mars the image, he stands for an intense, irrevocable pride of craft. Williams, after recounting one of the infrequent concessions Pound made, goes on:

"But that was only a momentary aberration
on the part of the grrrrrreatest poet drawing
breath in our day! And he meant it. That was
no joke to Ezra. He really lived the poet as few
of us had the nerve to live that exalted reality
in our time."[1]

It is extremely significant that Williams, whose style of life stands at the modest and conventional polar opposite of Pound's, speaks admiringly of Pound's nerve and of the poet's career as an "exalted reality." Perhaps as Pound's story unfolds, with its cargo of prejudice and betrayal, we shall come to see that his "really living" the role of poet is his chief merit in the eyes of his peers.

Pound's energy and activity were not limited to the fields of his acknowledged competence. He saw little distinction between a talent for art and a talent for social theory, and he equated art with all the rest of life in his adherence to the classical ideal of the artist as universal man. He had always been interested in the social world about him, and particularly in economic and political problems. He was violently opposed to the accumulation

---

[1] Norman, Charles: *op. cit.*, p. 50.

of money by shrewd but non-creative people, an anger perhaps not unrelated to the materially disprivileged circumstance of the artist. The question of control of money by the state was an obsession with him, and he strongly favored various "social credit" schemes. The great crime in Pound's eyes was that the wrong people controlled wealth and denied it to those more deserving. He wrote books and pamphlets, and spoke with gusto, in pursuing his economic theories. His seriousness was beyond doubt; he bombarded influential persons, including members of Congress and bankers, with his proposals. Although his ideas were probably not influential beyond a small circle of literary acolytes, they were vital to him. They were not logical, but were consistently infused with the money problem and the hatred of usury which was an *idée fixe*.

Pound's denunciation of usurers, in which he drew heavily from medieval documents, centered upon the notion that unjust, non-productive monetary gain lay at the root of modern economic and political ills. This polemical hobby-horse was neatly complemented by an important aspect of its author's personality: Pound was virulently anti-semitic. The stereotyped formula of Jew equals usurer equals evil came to dominate his thought.

His economic theories, which exalted the state as fiscal authority, linked with his anti-semitism to form a solid base for a growing affinity to fascism—specifically, to the corporate state of Mussolini. Several other strands in his fabric of values also prefigured a totalitarian design.

199

Pound felt rejected by the Western democracies, particularly by the United States, believing that they had betrayed the artist by leaving him unprotected from the market economy and the bland indifference of a mass audience. And underlying these various dispositions was one of the more pernicious of literary fallacies: the belief that the strict order and clarity of a well-formed work of art should somehow be recapitulated in the organization of human relations and the governing of men. As language must be kept clean and hard, so government should display an orderly hierarchy of unequivocal control. Pound's wanderings took him to Italy; for many years he lived at Rapallo, in isolation and in love with the country. The Italian state seemed to him as admirably efficient as a measured work of art. He came to admire the strongest Italian of them all, Benito Mussolini.

Soon Ezra Pound had an opportunity to put his fascistic devotion to direct use. Grown old and lonely in exile, and always a lover of flattery and recognition, he began to receive obeisance from more prominent sources than the citizens of Rapallo, who had called him "the poet" in whispered deference to his art. In return for the zeal he had demonstrated in such books as *Jefferson and/or Mussolini* ("I don't believe any estimate of Mussolini will be valid unless it *starts* from his passion for construction. Treat him as artifex [maker] and all the details fall into place. Take him as anything save the artist and you will get muddled with contradiction.") Pound was offered the use of the airwaves by Rome Radio.

200

"When war came, he was lending his voice, his erudition, and his bitterness against the United States, to further Italy's war effort.[1]

Pound's broadcasts over Rome Radio continued for several years. On the basis of the talks, he was considered a traitor to the United States, but since his trial has never been consummated he has not been found formally guilty of treason. The American government was prepared to prosecute; a group of his fellow-poets, asked to read transcripts of the broadcasts, affirmed that in their judgment Pound's intent had been treasonous. This opinion of his peers is from one point of view a very damaging verdict, since they may be presumed to have been sympathetic toward the recurrent aesthetic features of the broadcasts and favorable toward Pound's poetic reputation. The fact of his presumed guilt is not vitiated by the consideration that his efforts must have been exceedingly ineffective as Axis propaganda. His scripts are a rather jumbled mixture of literary criticism, anti-semitic venom, hero-worship of dictators, and the ordinary Axis propaganda line. Two selections from the broadcasts are available. One, favorable to Pound, consists of literary meanderings, including only a few sentences about dictators and virtually no anti-semitism.[2] The other contains standard fascist myth liberally punc-

---

[1] Norman, Charles: *op. cit.,* p. 37.
[2] Rudge, Olga: "If This Be Treason—" (*op. cit.*)

tuated with warnings of the type practiced by Axis Sally or Tokyo Rose, aimed at discouraging American troops about the worth of their contribution. For instance:

"Well, you have been fed on lies, for twenty years you have been fed on lies, and I don't say maybe. And Mr. Squirmy and Mr. Slime are still feeding it to you right over the B.B.C. radio, and everyone of the Jew radios of Schenectady, New York, and Boston—

"And how much liberty have you got, anyhow? And as to the arsenal—are you the arsenal of democracy or of judeocracy?"

"Every day of war is a dead day as well as a death day. More death, more future servitude, less and less of American liberty of any variety."

"Every hour that you go on with this war is an hour lost to you and your children. And every sane act you commit is committed in homage to Mussolini and Hitler."

"You ought not to be at war against Italy . . . You are doing it for the sake of a false accountancy system."[1]

All this, *ad nauseam,* is supplemented by very literate examinations of E. E. Cummings, James Joyce, and others, and by Pound's own poetry. Pound claimed he was acting in support of the Constitution of the United

---

[1] Norman, Charles: *op. cit.*

States, and that the Italian government never asked him to say anything "contrary to his duties as an American Citizen." What he called his "personal propaganda," in other words, merely happened to coincide with the official ideology of his country's enemies. While the broadcasts were being made, *Poetry* editorialized in outraged tones:

> "The time has come to put a formal end to the countenancing of Ezra Pound . . . That it should be one of the poets who is thus playing Lord Haw-Haw, no matter how ineffectually, seems to cast a slur on the whole craft. In the name of American poetry, and of all who practice the art, let us hope that this is the end of Ezra Pound."[1]

Indeed, *Poetry*'s contempt for Pound's irresponsible political behavior was widely shared among his fellow poets. But this was not "the end of Ezra Pound." The plot grew more complicated, for he did not die as a fascist traitor. He lived, was imprisoned, and, when at length hospitalized as incompetent, was given a prize.

Pound was arrested in May, 1945, and confined for some time to a prison camp in Italy, near Pisa. As a prisoner he continued to write poetry, producing a further number of the *Cantos* on which he had long been engaged. The new manuscript, written in pencil on

---

[1] Quoted in Norman, Charles: *op. cit.*

rough notepaper, was later to be published by *New
Directions* as *The Pisan Cantos,* and was to become one
of the most heatedly discussed volumes of poetry in our
time. Whatever his opinion of the aesthetic or moral
values in this book, any reader who examines the original manuscript will find it difficult to suppress a feeling
of awe before the compelling drive of Pound's creative
spirit. Soiled, creased pages attest to the penal environment in which it was composed: here is the poet at
work, exerting the will to form, shaping the material of
existence under a bleak and hostile circumstance.

After some time, Pound was returned to the United
States to stand trial for treason. He arrived in extremely
poor physical and mental condition, emaciated and tor-
mented. Awaiting trial, he was removed from the District
Jail, in Washington, D.C., to Gallinger Hospital for observation. The jury at his sanity hearing found him,
upon psychiatric testimony, to be of unsound mind. He
was removed soon afterward to St. Elizabeth's Hospital.
The examining psychiatrists reported:

> "At the present time he exhibits extremely
> poor judgment as to his situation, its seriousness
> and the manner in which the charges are to be
> met. He insists that his broadcasts were not
> treasonable, but that all of his radio activities
> have stemmed from his self-appointed mission
> to 'save the Constitution.' He is abnormally
> grandiose, is expansive and exuberant in man-

ner, exhibiting pressure of speech, discursiveness, and distractibility.

In our opinion, with advancing years his personality, for many years abnormal, has undergone further distortion to the extent that he is now suffering from a paranoid state which renders him mentally unfit to advise properly with counsel or to participate intelligently and reasonably in his own defense. He is, in other words, insane and mentally unfit for trial, and is in need of care in a mental hospital."[1]

The keystone of Pound's paranoia seems to be his anti-semitism; he is reported to have expressed great fear that, if ever released, he would be shot down at the hospital by the hated Jews. It is fairly apparent that from early manhood he had begun to evolve a proto-paranoid system marked by extreme ideas of personal grandeur and an acute sensitivity to real or imagined slights. Although some might identify delusions of grandeur as the favored disease of great poets, recalling Yeats' notions about his aristocratic lineage or considering the artist's need for a heightened confidence in self, even Pound eventually conceded that he experienced a certain mental difficulty. Stephen Spender writes of a visit to the hospital ward:

---

[1] Quoted in Norman, Charles: *op. cit.*

"I asked him [Pound] whether he remembered the visit of Yeats to Rapallo. He looked
at me and said: 'If you want me to talk about
Yeats I shall do so, but you must give me
twenty-four hours' notice, as the top layer of my
mind is gone.' "

Early in 1949, Ezra Pound was awarded the Bollingen
Prize for Poetry. The prize, donated by the Bollingen
Foundation, was given for the best book of poetry published during the preceding year, in this case *The Pisan
Cantos.* Judges for the award were the Fellows in American Letters of the Library of Congress, a group of distinguished writers including T. S. Eliot, Allen Tate,
Conrad Aiken, Robert Lowell, and several others of outstanding reputation. The judges were alert to the controversy which might ensue; such an award was certain
to provoke discussion, not only because of Pound's
status but because *The Pisan Cantos* themselves contained sections reiterating his anti-semitic and fascist
ideology. After recognizing that objections might be
raised, they ended a public statement with these words:

"To permit other considerations than that of
poetic achievement to sway the decision would
destroy the significance of the award and would
in principle deny the validity of that objective
perception of value on which any civilized society must rest."

Many poets have hinted that the Fellows voted the
prize in a spirit of defiance, as if determined to outrage

206

the public in return for their own disprivileged position in society. But although this sort of shocking counter-attack is occasionally a congenial indulgence for the artist, it does not represent a motivation serious enough to drive responsible professionals in a matter of first importance. Other comments imply that a core group of poets, some of them Fellows, decided some time before the judging to "do something for Pound" in view of his sorry plight. At any rate the judges convened with a strong pro-Pound sentiment already in motion. It is significant that at this point, before voting began, T. S. Eliot warned against giving the prize to *The Pisan Cantos*; he felt the action might do Pound more harm than good. The assembled poets, however, refused in this situation to accept the advice of a leader who is perhaps the most powerful of contemporary literary figures. Their major premise was that the book itself was superior to the other candidates and deserved the prize regardless of pressures arising outside the aesthetic framework of judgment. Underlying this premise was the desire to be loyal to a fellow-artist, and, probably, a certain need to challenge the Philistines.

The Pisan Cantos are of uneven quality; they are generally acknowledged to contain passages of rare beauty and also passages of viciously anti-Jewish tone. Of the latter:

"Pétain defended Verdun while Blum was defending a bidet."

"The yidd is a stimulant, and the goyim are

cattle in gt/proportion and go to saleable
slaughter with the maximum of docility."

A perfect critical consensus is of course impossible,
and there were many poets who thought the book un-
worthy, but on balance it seems true that the majority
of critical readers considered the volume prize-deserving
when compared with its competitors of that year. The
vital questions then become, first, whether the accomplishment of the chief poetic task outweighs lines like
those quoted above; and, second, whether it is proper to
honor a presumed traitor in the light of his book's excellence.

General reaction to the prize was not immediate, but
by the summer of 1949 the controversy had become a
public debate. William Barrett's editorial in the April
Partisan Review was followed in May by a panel of opinion from poets and critics. The major issues were here
joined, yet discussion had not become really widespread.
The problems had been kept within the family, and the
pros and cons upheld by members in good craft standing. Soon, however, the poet Robert Hillyer wrote two
exceedingly polemical articles, violently attacking Pound
and his prize, which were published in the *Saturday Review of Literature*. The circulation of the magazine and
the bitter temper of the essays combined to produce a
storm of angry argument. Congressmen demanded investigation, since the Fellows had been at least temporarily
identified with the Library of Congress.

The Hillyer articles, the first of which was entitled,

"Treason's Strange Fruit," opposed Pound and the Bollingen Prize on two main counts: the immorality of an award to a war criminal, and the alleged activity of a poetic clique which had foisted Pound and Eliot off on an unsuspecting audience. The prize was supposed to represent the last stage of a proto-fascist coup d'art, confirming the dictatorship of Pound and Eliot in the style and content of modern poetry. Using the now-familiar technique of guilt-by-association, Hillyer went to great lengths to implicate a variety of literary figures in the "plot." His antagonistic tone and his widening of the debate to include all of "modern poetry" as a target set off a great deal of protest. A group of one hundred poets, novelists, and critics signed a petition denouncing the *Saturday Review* for its editorial defense of Hillyer's articles. This group published a book, *The Case Against the Saturday Review of Literature*, in which they protested the magazine's stand and strongly countered Hillyer's thesis.

Hillyer's charges, and the reply to them, illustrate several aspects of poets' behavior as a group. Since Hillyer is himself a distinguished poet his attack aroused the most energetic and irate defense; defection from within is the worst possible crime to a marginal group which must constantly fight for the very life of its profession. Attack from without is to be expected, but there is a strong belief that poets should all hang together in order that they may versify separately. A similar logic applies to the condemnation of the *Saturday Review,* because there are in any event few enough journals to support the poet. Many writers protested that Hillyer's deprecation of modern poetry opened the gates to the Philistines, aiding the enemies of artistic experiment in a society where art is none too secure. The lively debate also pointed up the existence of numerous sub-groups within the general body of American poets. Many of these aggregations, especially the "traditionalists," had long been out of critical favor and jealous of the Eliot leadership. Hillyer thus became a rallying-point for the discontented, for those who bore some grudge against front-running trends in criticism and style. The Pound award focused intra-craft tensions which rest upon both genuine aesthetic differences and less principled clashes of personality.

Pound's career, particularly at the time of the prize, raises a central issue of the artist's relation to his society. How far may artistic merit override other considerations of the poet as citizen? But the question was not seen as primary by the majority of poets and critics who were involved. They tended to make the separation of the book from the man axiomatic, to maintain that poetic man and political man should be treated as mutually exclusive roles:

"Two things have to be, and are here distinguished: the case of Pound the man, and the value of the particular book, *The Pisan Cantos.* Pound the man has passed beyond the court of literary criticism into the jurisdiction of psy-

210

chiatry and public justice, and it would be gratuitously vindictive for anyone to heap new tribulation on his wretched figure. Therefore, our concern is, like that of the Bollingen judges, directly with the single book.

. . . The Pound case enables us to put it to aestheticians in this definite way:

How far is it possible, in a lyric poem, for technical embellishments to transform ugly and vicious matter into beautiful poetry?"[1]

This readiness to divorce the artistic role from other activities of the artist, so pronounced even in most individuals who were in some degree critical of the award, is perhaps the most enlightening revelation of the Pound debate. It indicates that the technical specialization characteristic of modern Western society is accepted as an accomplished fact of life by the very persons who have traditionally insisted on a concept of the "whole man": the artists themselves. The general defense of the separation of powers and judgments underlying the award is not quite "art for art's sake," although it has affinities with such a philosophy. Rather, it is an affirmation of certain basic attitudes governing achievement and vocational virtuosity in American culture. The questions become: not who Pound is, but what poems he achieved;

---

[1] Barrett, William: "A Prize for Ezra Pound," *Partisan Review,* April, 1949.

not a total response to Pound the person, but a restricted estimate of one of his technical displays. One might say that in the long run this must always be the posture of those who deal with the arts, since all that remains at last is the poem. The writer's partisan entanglements in the life of his times, and even his deepest human relationships, are erased or at least faded by the dust of centuries. What is perhaps remarkable is the adoption of this timeless stance in the heat of a contemporary situation.

Although no one has taken a vote, it is safe to conclude that a very substantial portion, perhaps a majority, of this country's first-rate poets supported the Pound prize. Whether or not they liked *The Pisan Cantos,* they felt it was crucial to emphasize the separation of art and state as a guiding principle. They feared that to deny the prize on grounds extrinsic to artistic merit would open the door to censorship, to demands that the poet be politically pure. The enforced ideology of Soviet writers was prominent in their apprehensions. American poets hold tenaciously to their independence, demanding of society above all else that it leave them alone.

If the separation of artist from citizen is the major lesson in values to be drawn from the way his fellow poets regard Ezra Pound, certainly another important feature is the exaltation of the poet's role. Ezra Pound, whatever his deficiencies, had "really lived" the poet. In an age when poetry is not revered and the poet may at best devote part time to his work, there are inevitably

212

overtones of grandeur about a man who was so resoundingly the artist for better or worse, in public and private. Obviously, too, the act of thrusting Pound into a niche of public honor at a time when he had been so apparently cast down by his society is a defiant slap at the power of the conforming majority.

In addition to the conflicts within the total poetic community which were magnified by the Hillyer articles and their consequences, tensions became plain even within the *avant-garde* of critically favored experimental poets. Those who applauded the prize often did so for quite different reasons. Although poets may draw together under attack, their highly personal attitudes and differing aesthetic-critical tenets are never entirely submerged. The Fellows were not themselves unanimous in voting the award:

> "I voted against Pound in the belief that the poet's political and moral philosophy ultimately vitiates his poetry and lowers its standards as literary work."[1]

Karl Shapiro also outlines the way in which Pound's position as a leader among poets, and his distinct force of personality, may have brought criteria outside the strictly aesthetic sphere to bear on the selection:

> "The jury that elected Pound was made up

---

[1] Shapiro, Karl, in "The Question of the Pound Award," *Partisan Review*, May, 1949.

213

partly of Pound's contemporaries, those who
had come under his influence as impressario
and teacher, those who had at some time made
declarations of political reaction, and those who
had engaged in the literary struggle to dissociate art from social injunction. The presence of
Mr. Eliot at the meeting gave these facts a reality which perhaps inhibited open discussion.
For reasons of personal loyalty, which one must
respect, and for reasons of sectarian literary
loyalty, which one may or may not respect, few
poets are in a position to say what they really
think of Pound's work."[1]

Pound and his prize are symbols of the poet's wish to
declare himself apolitical. After a period, most importantly during the 1930's, in which "social significance"
was often demanded of the writer, we have come to a
phase in which political-artistic nuances are unfashion-
able. The modern poet does not desire, and does not
believe, that his work should be without a deep social
import to his fellow men, but he refuses to link poetry
to the transient political and social currents of a particular time. Poetry is not propaganda, and as political conformity increases in the United States under the pressures
of prosperity and anti-Communism the poet does not
want to get in line *as artist*. He has other and to him

---

[1] *Ibid.*

214

more lasting things to do. Some poets go even further than announcing that their poetry is on another level of life than politics and the daily affairs of nations. They cheer Pound as an international man of pure value whose work and life escape the claims of national loyalty. Like his beloved Dante, as Charles Olson has said, Pound succeeded in becoming a political outcast; did he thereby become a harbinger of pure poetic value? Does the paranoid-traitor in his misery exemplify a return to a pre-nationalistic state of grace, in which the poet renounces citizenship and sings on in lonely splendor?

Despite what might have been the prophetic yearning in those lines of *The Pisan Cantos*—

"Down, Derry-down

Oh let an old man rest."

—Ezra Pound has continued a surprisingly active life in art. From his hospital sanctuary he has exerted a weakened but visible leadership, especially among younger writers. He has written, translated, criticized, and all in all made the best of his cabined situation. Repudiated by his country and renounced by many of his oldest literary friends, he has kept working. Pound's poetic vitality in a frame of disgrace and degeneration has been a profound instance of the creative man's unending drive toward self-realization.

A further chapter in Ezra Pound's career is now beginning. Largely through the intervention of fellow poets, including some like Robert Frost who can by no means be numbered among his admirers, the Government has

215

agreed not to press the treason charges. St. Elizabeth's Hospital authorities discharged Pound, "condition not improved," on May 7, 1958, and he has returned to Italy. One can only guess at his influence on the poetry of the next few years or at his own probable creative achievements. His return to civil life after thirteen years' confinement attests at the very least to the artist's tough, persistent grasp on the real world and to the potency of artistic fellowship.

BIBLIOGRAPHY

BOOKS

Aiken, Conrad. *Ushant*. New York and Boston. Duell, Sloan & Pearce, Inc.; Little, Brown and Co., 1952

Allport, Gordon W. *Becoming*. New Haven: Yale University Press, 1955

Personality. New York: Henry Holt & Co., Inc., 1937

Auden, W. H. *Nones*. New York: Random House, 1951

Bergler, Edmund. *The Writer and Psychoanalysis*. Garden City: Doubleday & Co., Inc., 1950

Bodkin, Maud. *Archetypal Patterns in Poetry*. London: Oxford University Press, Inc., 1934

Carlyle, Thomas. *On Heroes, Hero Worship and the Heroic in History*. London: Chapman and Hall, 1840

Coleridge, Samuel Taylor. *Biographia Literaria*. New York: E. P. Dutton & Co., Inc., 1908

Dahlberg, Edward. *Do These Bones Live?* New York: Harcourt, Brace & Co., 1941

Eliot, T. S. *The Sacred Wood*. London: Methuen & Co., Ltd., 1920

The Use of Poetry and the Use of Criticism. Cambridge: Harvard University Press, 1933

Emerson, Ralph Waldo. *The Complete Works of——*. Boston: Houghton, 1903-1904

Empson, William, *Seven Types of Ambiguity*. New York: Oxford University Press, 1947

Erikson, Erik H. *Childhood and Society*. New York: W. W. Norton & Co., Inc., 1950

Freud, Sigmund. "The Relation of the Poet to Day-dreaming," *Collected Papers*, IV. London: Hogarth Press and the Institute of Psychoanalysis, 1925

Frost, Robert. "The Figure a Poem Makes," Introduction to *Collected Poems of Robert Frost*. New York: Henry Holt & Co., Inc., 1939

Heller, Erich. *The Hazard of Modern Poetry*. Cambridge: Bowes and Bowes Publishers, Ltd., 1953

Huizinga, Johan. *Homo Ludens*. Boston: Beacon Press Inc., 1955

Hutchinson, E. D. "The Nature of Insight" and "The Period of Frustration in Creative Endeavor," in *A Study of Interpersonal Relations*, ed. Patrick Mullahy. New York: Hermitage Press, 1949

Johnson, Samuel. *The Lives of the Most Eminent English Poets*. London: Methuen & Co., Ltd., 1896

Josephson, Matthew. *Portrait of the Artist as American*. New York: Harcourt, Brace & Co., 1930

Jung, C. G. *Modern Man in Search of a Soul*. New York: Harcourt, Brace & Co., 1933

Kretschmer, Ernst. *The Psychology of Men of Genius*. New York: Harcourt, Brace and Co., 1931

Kroeber, Alfred L. *Configurations of Culture Growth.* Berkeley: University of California Press, 1944

Langer, Suzanne K. *Philosophy in a New Key.* Cambridge: Harvard University Press, 1942

Leach, E. R. "Æsthetics," *The Institutions of Primitive Society.* Glencoe, Ill.: The Free Press, 1954

Lewis, M. M. *Language in Society.* London: Thomas Nelson & Sons, 1947

Lowes, J. L. *The Road to Xanadu.* Boston: Houghton Mifflin Co., 1930

MacLeish, Archibald. "Ars Poetica" and "Invocation to the Social Muse," *Collected Poems, 1917-1952.* Boston: Houghton Mifflin Co., 1952

Mid-Century American Poets. Edited by John Ciardi. New York: Twayne Publishers, 1950

Milosz, Czeslaw. *The Captive Mind.* New York: Alfred A. Knopf, Inc., 1953

Moore, Marianne. "Poetry," *Collected Poems.* New York: The Macmillan Co., 1951

Morris, Charles. *Signs, Language, and Behavior.* New York: Prentice-Hall, Inc., 1946

Murray, Henry A. "Introduction" in Burton, Arthur, and Harris, Robert E., *Case Histories in Clinical and Abnormal Psychology.* New York: Harper & Brothers, 1947

Norman, Charles. *The Case of Ezra Pound.* New York: The Bodley Press, 1948

Ogden, C. K., and Richards, I. A. *The Meaning of Meaning.* 5th ed. New York: Harcourt, Brace & Co., 1938

Poets at Work. Introduction by Charles D. Abbott. New York: Harcourt, Brace & Co., 1948. [Contains writing by W. H. Auden, R. Arnheim, K. Shapiro, and D. Stauffer.]

Pollock, T. C. *The Nature of Literature.* Princeton: Princeton University Press, 1942.

Pound, Ezra. *Patria Mia.* Chicago: Ralph Fletcher Seymour, 1950

Personae. New York: New Directions, 1949

The Pisan Cantos. New York: New Directions, 1948

Quiller-Couch, Sir Arthur. *The Poet as Citizen.* New York: The Macmillan Co., 1935

Rank, Otto. *Art and Artist.* New York: Alfred A. Knopf, Inc., 1932

Read, Herbert. *Phases of English Poetry.* "The Direction Series." Norfolk, Conn.: James Laughlin, 1951

Richards, I. A. *Science and Poetry.* London: Kegan Paul, Trench, Trubner and Co., Ltd., 1935

Rosenzweig, Saul. "The Ghost of Henry James," in *Personality in Nature, Society, and Culture,* ed. Clyde Kluckhohn, Henry A. Murray, and David M. Schneider. 2nd ed. New York: Alfred A. Knopf, Inc., 1953

Rudge, Olga. *"If This Be Treason—".* Sienna: Tip. Nuova, 1948

Schneider, Daniel E. *The Psychoanalyst and the Artist.* New York: Farrar, Straus and Cudahy, Inc., 1950

Simmel, Georg. "The Metropolis and Mental Life," in *The Sociology of Georg Simmel,* ed. K. Wolff. Glencoe, Ill.: The Free Press, 1950

Speier, Hans. "Shakespeare's *The Tempest,*" *Social Order and the Risks of War.* New York: George W. Stewart Publisher, Inc., 1952

Spencer, Theodore. "A Reason for Writing," *The Paradox in the Circle.* New York: New Directions, 1941

Spender, Stephen. "The Making of a Poem," in *Critiques and Essays in Criticism, 1920-1948,* ed. R. W. Stallman. New York: Ronald Press, 1949
World Within World. New York: Harcourt, Brace & Co., 1951

Stallman, R. W., ed. *Critiques and Essays in Criticism: 1920-1948.* New York: The Ronald Press Company, 1949

Trilling, Lionel. *The Liberal Imagination.* New York: The Viking Press, Inc., 1950

Wilson, Edmund. *The Wound and the Bow.* Boston: Houghton Mifflin Co., 1941

Whyte, L. L. *The Next Development in Man.* New York: Henry Holt & Co., Inc., 1948

Yeats, W. B. *The Collected Poems of——.* New York: The Macmillan Co., 1951

Zipf, George K. *The Psychobiology of Language.* Boston: Houghton Mifflin Co., 1935

PERIODICALS

Albrecht, M. C. "Psychological Motives in the Fiction of Julian Green," *Journal of Personality,* March, 1948

Allport, Gordon W. "Personality: A Problem for Science or a Problem for Art?", *Revista de Psihologie,* 1938

Barr, Donald. Review of Joyce Cary's *The Horse's Mouth, New York Times Book Review,* January 29, 1950

Barrett, William. "A Prize for Ezra Pound," *Partisan Review,* April, 1949

Burrow, Trigant. "The Social Neurosis: A Study in 'Clinical Anthropology,'" *Philosophy of Science,* January, 1949

Ciardi, John. "The Morality of Poetry," *The Saturday Review,* March 30, 1957

Erikson, Erik H. "The Problem of Ego-Identity," *Journal of the American Psychoanalytic Association,* January, 1956

Lee, Harry B. "On the Esthetic States of the Mind," *Psychiatry,* August, 1947

Lowenthal, Leo and Fiske, Marjorie. "Reaction to Mass Media Growth in Eighteenth Century England," *Journalism Quarterly,* Fall, 1956

"The Question of the Pound Award," *Partisan Review,* May, 1949. (Comments by Auden, Davis, Greenberg, Howe, Orwell, Shapiro, Tate, and Barrett)

Romney, Barbara. "Prospectus for a New Publication: *Poetry Broadside,*" New York: 1957

Schachtel, Ernest. "On Memory and Childhood Amnesia," *Psychiatry,* February, 1947

Thomas, Dylan. "How To Be A Poet," *Atlantic Monthly,* July 1951

Turnell, Martin. "The Writer and Social Strategy," *Partisan Review*, March-April, 1951

Wilson, Robert N. "Aesthetic Symbolism," *American Imago*, Fall, 1955. "Poetic Creativity," *Psychiatry*, May, 1954. "Literature, Society, and Personality," *Journal of Aesthetics and Art Criticism*, June, 1952

Robert N. Wilson, *a native of up-state New York, was educated at Union College, (B.A., 1948) and Harvard University, (Ph.D., 1952). Following military service in the European theatre he matriculated at Trinity Hall, Cambridge (England). Subsequently he has been a member of the staff of the Harvard Psychological Clinic, the Cornell University faculty, the staff of the Social Science Research Council, and a Fellow at The Center for Advanced Study in the Behavioral Sciences at Stanford.*

In 1957 Mr. Wilson was appointed a Lecturer on Sociology in the Division of Psychiatry of the Harvard Medical School. He also teaches Sociology in Harvard's Department of Social Relations.

Mr. Wilson is a contributor to the Antioch Review, Psychiatry, American Imago, Human Organization, *and the* Journal of Aesthetics and Art Criticism. *He is co-author, with Temple Burling and Edith Lentz, of* The Give and Take in Hospitals (G. P. Putnam's Sons, 1956) *and co-editor, with Alexander H. Leighton and John A. Clausen, of* Explorations in Social Psychiatry (Basic Books, Inc., 1957).

THE TYPOGRAPHY, PRINTING, AND BINDING
OF THIS BOOK WERE EXECUTED BY
JACKSON TYPESETTING COMPANY OF JACKSON, MICHIGAN
CUSHING-MALLOY INC., LITHOGRAPHERS, OF ANN ARBOR
AND WILLIAM B. EERDMANS COMPANY OF GRAND RAPIDS
THE TEXT IS SET IN 10 POINT BASKERVILLE
AND THE HEADINGS IN 18 POINT GARAMOND